GARDEN STONE

GARDEN STONE

Creative Ideas, Practical Projects, and
Inspiration for Purely Decorative Uses

BARBARA PLEASANT

PHOTOGRAPHY BY DENCY KANE

STOREY BOOKS

North Adams
Massachusetts

The mission of Storey Publishing is to serve our customers by publishing practical information that encourages personal independence in harmony with the environment.

Edited by Gwen W. Steege and Larry Shea
Cover design and interior art direction by Wendy Palitz
Cover photography by Dency Kane
Illustrations by Kathy Kester
Interior design by Tom Morgan, Blue Design
Book layout and production by Mark Tomasi, Cindy McFarland, and Susan Bernier
Indexed by Eileen M. Clawson

The information in this book is true and complete to the best of our knowledge. All recommendations are made without guarantee on the part of the author or Storey Publishing. The author and publisher disclaim any liability in connection with the use of this information. For additional information please contact Storey Books, 210 MASS MoCA Way, North Adams, MA 01247.

Storey Books are available for special premium and promotional uses and for customized editions. For further information, please call Storey's Custom Publishing Department at 1-800-793-9396.

Printed in China by C & C Offset Printing Co., Ltd.
10 9 8 7 6 5 4 3 2 1

Library of Congress Cataloging-in-Publication Data

Pleasant, Barbara
    Garden Stone : creative ideas, practical projects, and inspiration for purely decorative uses / by Barbara Pleasant.
        p. cm
    Includes bibliographical references (p.) and index.
    ISBN 1-58017-406-X (alk. paper)
    1. Stone in landscape gardening.   I. Title.

SB475.5 .P54 2002
717—dc21   2001049248

Creating a book is supposed to be torturously hard work, but this one was pure pleasure. We wish to thank the many generous gardeners and garden designers who shared their private worlds with us, our loved ones for their steadfast support, and our gifted editors for attending to a thousand small details.

— Barbara Pleasant and Dency Kane

CONTENTS

introduction	Using Stone in the Garden	8
chapter 1	Garden Visions in Stone	14
chapter 2	Pathways with Purpose	44
chapter 3	Making Assets of Hills and Dips	78
chapter 4	The Romance of Stone Walls	100
chapter 5	Rock Gardening with Stone	132
chapter 6	Stone, Water & Gardens	160
chapter 7	Garden Ornaments	190
chapter 8	Working with Stone	212
	Resources	230
	USDA Zone Map	232
	Index	234

USING STONE IN THE GARDEN

When a garden includes stone, you can almost hear the stone's gentle rumble. Emerging from  the depths of the earth, stone is a visible reminder of the very origins of our planet. Its power derives from its apparent permanence, and yet stone is constantly changing. Used creatively, stone turns us into movers of mountains and students of the passage of time. This is the essence of gardening with stone.

Sedums wander tapestry–like wherever they can catch a foothold, while achillea and goatsbeard provide height and splashes of color.

An Eternal Relationship

Which came first, the garden or the stone? Wherever plants and stone coexist, the question confronts and teases us, until we realize that either answer can be correct. This is both the promise and the challenge of gardening with stone: to create spaces that marry the profound permanence of stone with the seasonal cycles of death and rebirth so eloquently represented by plants.

Like plants, stone in the garden can be dramatic or tranquil, logical or surprising, somber or whimsical. We can see stories unfold through the stones left behind, for example, when we find plants surviving in the midst of the ruins from an old house wall or chimney that has crumbled into the garden that surrounded it. A scree garden created on a stone outcropping can amplify nature's innate tensions among wind, rock, and life in much the same way that a water run lined with smooth stones reflects the sculpting power of water. A special arrangement of stones can venerate a place, making it sacred, or it can simply celebrate the human imagination that lays out stones in dreamlike patterns.

Herein lies the art of gardening with stone. As with other forms of art, a garden that includes stone becomes more than the sum of its parts, just as a Monet painting is far more than pigment on canvas or a Shakespeare sonnet conveys much more than mere words and their dictionary meanings. On a simple level, stone in the garden is beautiful, but it imparts more than just color, texture, and line. When used artfully, stone simply belongs, absolutely and intrinsically, wherever it is placed. When the synchrony is perfect, plants growing in the company of stone appear completely natural and at home.

It takes decades for lichens to paint patterns on the stones of a weathered wall (LEFT) but only a few seasons to create the fireworks provided by these towering delphinium and fragrant red roses.

A mound of Siberian iris (RIGHT) echoes the spreading form of a large shade tree silhouetted behind large, smooth boulders. Plants with upright forms and grassy textures tend to lighten the heavy presence of stone.

The Perfectly Practical and the Purely Decorative

It's a happy coincidence that stone can be purely decorative or can be used to make a garden more accessible and easy to maintain. Yet even at its most practical — guiding your steps up a slope, channeling water away from your door, or holding back a hillside — stone can and should be thought of as durable garden art. When you make anything out of stone, you exercise both body and soul, and the processes involved are much more than mechanical. Indeed, you cannot complete the first step, selecting stone, without conjuring up a vision of what you want to create and then using your eyes and hands to examine, touch, and test stones for suitability. It's possible that you will run across stone that is not right for the project you have in mind but that you realize would be perfect for something else. If you let it, stone will lead you to its best use, and this rightness of positioning will show in your finished work.

This book includes hundreds of ideas for using stone in your garden. Most of the projects involve working with stone that is not extremely heavy, so you can do many of them yourself with only a little help. My purpose here is to help gardeners enjoy the magic of working with stone, which is far different from teaching the hard-learned skills of a stonemason or helping you design massive projects that require heavy equipment, hundreds of man-hours, and thousands of dollars. Rather, I want to help you discover a new realm of creativity in your gardening life in which stone, plants, soil, water, and light interact with your knowledge and your imagination so that your garden evolves into a place of enduring beauty.

A stone-rimmed raised bed for pretty lettuce and other edibles (FAR LEFT) may be so attractive that you hesitate to gather the harvest.

Equally practical, a single slab of stone (LEFT) creates a sturdy bridge across a woodland stream.

Ensconced at the base of a slope clothed in evergreen shrubs (ABOVE), a stone sitting area basks in the refreshing fragrance of lavender. Daylilies and rudbeckia beckon human and butterfly visitors to explore the riches of this special destination.

In Japanese tradition, a twine-wrapped stone (RIGHT) signals that this path should not be used.

CHAPTER 1

GARDEN VISIONS IN STONE

What do you want stone to do for your garden? Or, more fundamentally, what kind of place do you want your garden to be? To answer, you must know  yourself well enough to know what you want, and you must know enough about the endless possibilities available when making a garden. As you pick up clues slowly over time, you will discover workable visions, large and small, of ways to use stone to sculpt the garden of your dreams.

Imagination, inspired by the ways other gardeners — and nature itself — have used stone, can lead to pleasing combinations, like this handsome retaining wall softened by *Iris laevigata*, acorus, and other moisture-loving plants.

Designing with Stone

When you are planning and designing a garden with stone, your inspiration begins from two very different places. One point of origin is the eternal nature of stone itself; the other is the art of landscape design as expressed by a variety of cultures over many hundreds of years.

Whether your garden is relatively new or very old, visually connecting and coordinating the various areas of your landscape requires a balance of practical needs and aesthetic goals. You can accomplish this through several tried-and-true principles of landscape design. Because stone is such an excellent material for solving practical problems, such as a lack of pathways or a preponderance of slippery slopes, it makes sense to first examine how you might use stone to make your gar-

den more accessible and easier to maintain. Do you need a broad landing outside an entryway or a safe corridor to link your house and your garden? Parts of your property that flood may deserve a higher priority, but in general, people like to get their entryways in shape before developing other parts of the landscape.

Go Native

While you are studying ways you might decide to incorporate stone in your garden and landscape, you should also be investigating what kind of stone is available in your area. I always prefer native stone, both because it is more economical and because it fits more naturally into any site where it is used.

A gravel pathway wide enough for two people to walk side by side gives a narrow corridor a spacious feeling (LEFT). Rhythmically placed containers provide height without crowding, and they help exaggerate the length of the passage.

Weathered fieldstone makes for relaxed movement through a shady woodland garden (RIGHT). Wide places where the stonework extends into the garden invite further exploration. In keeping with natural processes, occasional plants are encouraged to find footholds between the stones.

Whether you are improving an entryway to add to your home's curb appeal or just having fun creating a unique stonescape in your backyard, the choices of materials and designs are all up to you, of course. Whatever you endeavor to do, I must urge you to do it with a wonderful sense of style. This is a fluid concept that is difficult to pin down, particularly in the eclectic world of contemporary gardening, but I do like Webster's description of style as "distinctive excellence" to summarize how it is achieved through appropriate yet original choice and arrangement of various elements.

Of Stone and Style

Throughout history, wherever people have lived in close company with stone, they have developed landscaping styles that use stone to create special moods, to strengthen the link between the human and the divine, or to delve into the natural tensions that exist among earth, sky, and water. If you wish to, you can re-create any of a number of distinctive historical styles, or you can create a style of your own.

It may be tempting to borrow bits and pieces from varying schools of style. This is fine as long as you don't lose touch with the strong element of continuity that stone can bring to your landscape. Stone features made of indigenous stone tie the man-made and natural landscapes together with their color and texture, creating a measure of visual flow. You don't want to risk this benefit by combining stone features that are totally unrelated to each other in terms of style. For example, it is probably unwise to juxtapose primitive stonework against extremely ornate, civilized scenes. In similar fashion, you are asking for trouble if you go with a very stark, modern desert style, only to embellish it with fanciful rococo details borrowed from 18th-century France. That much said, let's look at a few distinctive cultural styles that may get your creative juices flowing.

Chinese Causation

Chinese gardening dramatizes natural forces and their causes and effects. Boulders and large stones with bold shapes and contours are often prominent features in Chinese gardens, suggesting the fundamental life forces that shape mountains into sand and the energies that surround and encompass all things as one. Even when Chinese gardens are scaled down to fit into small, enclosed courtyards, the intrinsic energy of stone is so important that the gardener may spend many weeks, months, or even years deciding on its best use and placement.

Plants carry out both aesthetic and ethical values, such as the necessity of humility, patience, and respect for nature. And because the Chinese culture is so ancient and rich in lore, individual species ranging from cherry blossoms to chrysanthemums can fill every square inch of the garden with meaning.

The quiet, earthy gray of this traditional farmhouse (LEFT) harmonizes well with the primitive stone slabs of the rock garden.

Wild forces of wind, water, gravity, and time are exaggerated in this Chinese garden (ABOVE), where each crevice is filled with delightful surprises.

Japanese Simplicity

Symbolism replaces realism in Japanese landscape gardens, though this is a symbolism sensitively handled. It must not overpower the ultimate goal, which is to make the garden feel like a very natural and tranquil place. The five essential elements are large rocks to simulate mountains, smaller smooth stones to symbolize moving rivers, water to suggest sea, tall plants to conjure forests, and open space and smaller plants to mimic fields. When it comes to the placement of the stones, asymmetrical balance is often the guiding energy, with large stones carefully placed in groups so that they almost resemble a family. A Japanese garden is very much situated on the earth, with strong emphasis placed on the surface plane. It is intended to be a place for sitting quietly, contemplating the inevitable passage of time.

Japanese gardens fall into two broad categories: rock gardens and landscape gardens. Japanese rock gardens include few, if any, plants; except for a few trees or shrubs, they derive all of their form and content from stone, gravel, and small ornaments and seating. Japanese landscape gardening, on the other hand, lets plants impart richness and meaning to the space in harmonious balance with stone.

The tranquility of a Japanese landscape garden (LEFT) is achieved through a magical blend of elements: forest, sea, open space, and boulders that suggest mountains.

These stepping-stones within a gravel-covered incline (ABOVE) are planned with sure footing and contemplation in mind. Repeating textures of wood and stone unify the scene.

Renaissance Revival

High-energy mosaics, elaborate sculpture, and much of what we now take for granted as the fundamental principles guiding the use of color can be traced to the suddenly freed imaginations of Renaissance artists. And although there is no single garden style that could encompass the variety of this dynamic period in the history of art, many of the small adornments that you might create with stone carry with them a whisper of old European inspiration. Fanciful patterning of stone pathways or walls hails from this period, as do circular rose gardens outlined with cut stone, formal fountains with elegant or whimsical sculptures, and specimen stones shaped into globes with small clipped shrubs to match.

Sculpted figures dance among impatiens behind a low stone wall (LEFT).

Random patterns of flagstone (RIGHT) play against the formality of manicured boxwoods.

Contemporary Spirit of Rebirth

You can use the spirit of renaissance in your garden without attempting to link it to any historical period. Strictly speaking, renaissance means "rebirth," and small stone features in the garden that suggest youthfulness, playful energy, or whimsical inventiveness can be expressions of the personal epiphanies we experience when we become deeply involved in our gardens. To me, a small pile of stones along a pathway that points in the direction one should go is a renaissance touch, as is a shallow stone bowl that is set where it will be warmed by the morning sun and become a magnet to basking butterflies. ■

American Naturalism

The strength and majesty of hills and mountains encrusted with natural stone are inescapable, so those of us who live surrounded by such landscapes cannot help but approach nature gently, with respect for the blueprint that has already been laid out before us. This becomes an almost romantic relationship as we seek to enhance the space around us, taming it only to the extent necessary to make our landscapes accommodate our passion for growing the plants we love. On sloping land, secure steps that enable us to reach inaccessible spaces are a logical addition, along with low walls that create plantable terraces among massive boulders. In many ways, gardening in rocky mountains and foothills is a sculpting process in which we carve our way toward planting pockets. In these situations, we often need to open windows in the overhead canopy of branches to get the sunshine needed to enrich our gardens with color, fragrance, and perhaps good things to eat.

Flat terrain marked by the slow trails of glaciers is often rich in evocative natural stonescapes as well. Patterns of rubble suggest meandering movement over level land, so you may seek to reinforce this characteristic with curving beds or soothing streambeds lined with stone. Native stone in glaciated areas is often of such manageable size that opportunities abound to work with cobble — small stones that are infinitely pile-able and pave-able and are often readily available in a rainbow of colors and textures.

In any area that is naturally rich with stone, you can develop a beautiful garden with an uncontrived appearance by sticking close to what your eyes and

Leathery rhododendrons are always beautiful partners for stone (LEFT). In a scene adopted from mountain woodlands, small rounded stone forms an easily managed staircase.

mind are prepared to accept as natural. In the eastern woodlands or the Pacific Northwest this means incorporating shade into your garden and celebrating the color green in its many different hues. On northern prairies, noble native grasses deserve emphasis, as do stone features that suggest steadfastness in the face of wind or that give almost supernatural life to accumulated snow.

Indestructible once established, creeping juniper (RIGHT) often grows in deep crevices between stones, a talent it derives from its ancestors in the mountains of Japan and British Columbia.

Desert Stone

When the searing sun of arid climates meets the impenetrable texture of stone, shadows are created, so that the interplay between light and darkness becomes an integral part of the garden scene. Large rocks are most dramatic, but piles of smaller stones can create similar special effects. The spiky texture of yuccas and other dry-climate plants with pointed leaves always contrasts well with rounded stones, while more jagged rocks provide fertile visual fodder for cacti and other succulents.

In extreme desert climates, stones often develop unusual colors on their outer layer, so that they appear reddish brown, black, orange, or gray, even though the stone interior may be buff tan. This phenomenon, called desert varnish, is due to the proliferation of bacteria and algae within thin layers of fungi. These are true lichens when ample moisture is available to support algae, but in the hottest, driest deserts, it's the bacteria that do the best job of surviving on sunbaked stone. Over a period of thousands of years, the bacteria cause a satiny patina to develop on exposed stone, which sometimes appears to have been blackened and glazed by fire. Used as specimens in a garden, these naturally varnished stones represent the true nature of the ancient desert. ■

Pursuing a Vision

The art and craft of gardening is a thoughtful process that compels us to balance the ecological realities of a site with its undeveloped possibilities, develop a plan, and then put that plan into action. Do not underestimate what you can do when you let your imagination delve deeply into the marriage of plants and stone. Perhaps you want a place that feels like a private sanctuary, or a more open garden room that sweeps you away with its classic elegance. You can use stone by itself or in combination with plants to create floors or walls, define lines, and set the mood for the place you want to create. Every step of the way, you should remain alert to the companionable connections that develop between plants and stone, because that's the source of the enchantment that you seek.

The Challenge of Scale

Wherever you find one stone in nature, you usually find many more. Small stones are formed by the breakup of larger ones, so nearby stones are inherently related. In your garden, you can re-create these relationships by placing stone features of varying sizes in positions that make them appear to have always existed exactly as they are. Then add carefully chosen plants to tie the stone family together or perhaps to accentuate the ways in which it divides into pieces.

Does this mean that you must include multiton boulders in your landscape? Not necessarily, though huge stones always add the sheer strength of their presence. Working with boulders is difficult and dangerous, so most of us have this done by landscaping

Bulwarks of large, flat stones frame a sitting area (LEFT). Enclosures structured with stone offer warmth and protection from wind for both plants and people.

A grove of trees is anchored by a family of boulders that tumble down a low berm (RIGHT). The berm provides ample space for planting moss and delicate deciduous ferns.

Closely set stepping-stones (LEFT) thread through a mixed border to an unseen garden ahead.

Circular cut stone steps (RIGHT) become a focal point for the change in elevation between two areas of lawn.

contractors or skilled stonemasons. But if you have no boulders and don't want to invest in them, a few tricks will enable you to get the big-rock, little-rock sense of scale that boulders impart.

Stone structures that include deep curves or circles can mimic the way boulders emerge from the ground as large, usually circular protuberances. Besides serving as a boulderlike visual mass, rounded stone features tend to make a place feel more comfortable. Especially when centrally located, a deeply curved or circular bed edged in stone, a patio of stones laid in a subtle radial pattern, or a water feature with lobed or circular edges becomes a natural nexus around which the rest of the garden can revolve.

Circles and curves are invaluable in small yards and in yards with natural slopes, and they can bring an air of intimacy to large properties, too. Yet the more space you have, the more possibilities you will discover for using stone to bring a feeling of movement to your landscape. For example, a series of stones that meander or tumble in one direction naturally carries you along with it. Or a stone walkway

that steps up or down into another section of your landscape immediately calls attention to the change, which you can exploit further if the steps coincide with a change of mood between balanced formality and more rustic surroundings.

The Finest Lines

When you use stone to pave a walkway or to build a low wall, it defines the lines of your landscape. Lines can lead you to various pleasurable destinations, such as a water feature, flower garden, or simply your front door, or they can be more visual in impact, showing your eyes where to look. In a very flat site, it will seem natural to use straight lines, which will in turn give your landscape a very clean, organized appearance. On the other hand, curves impart a feeling of mystery and movement appropriate in backyards, where we tend to spend time relaxing in private. Slopes that are already structured by natural stone can be tamed with broad curves, or you can make them dramatic with acute bows and bulges that accentuate the wildness of the natural terrain.

When Plants Meet Stone

As a gardener, you are always thinking on two levels at once when you are dreaming up plans for your landscape. You're thinking of plants you want to grow and the scene they will create when comfortably ensconced in stone. Will subtle patterns be enough, or do you want dramatic special effects? Serenity and quiet harmony, or the suggestion of eruptive violence? Blooming plants, in particular, can be extremely suggestive. Soft, quiet flower colors impart a feeling of peace, while hot reds and oranges sizzle with excitement.

The same is true with stone. Rounded, weathered stone always appears more settled and relaxed than jagged broken pieces. Stone is evocative. It can carry you away to craggy peaks of distant mountains, take you close to the bones of the earth, or hint at the presence of a meandering brook or bubbling spring. Pair stone with plants that carry similar messages: lean pines or Japanese maples that appear to have been shaped by mountain winds; cacti and succulents that hug rocky outcroppings; or ferns and woodland wildflowers typically found near lowland streams. The combined effect is so convincing that stepping out into your yard can feel like a journey to a faraway place, or an escape into a very intimate one.

The surface texture of stone is so different from the leafy lushness of plants that each tends to have a clarifying effect on the other. A collection of vegetables, herbs, or other edibles often appears more abundant when framed in stone beds, and the sensuous depth of roses is magnified by stonework at the plants' feet. The very wetness of water is intensified when framed in stone, and plants with fine-textured foliage seem even more dainty when settled in the company of flat or gently undulating stone.

Even when the plants are not in bloom, the pointed foliage of bearded iris (FACING PAGE) forms a beautiful skirt at the base of large stones.

A simple stone frame surrounds the mirror of this reflecting pool (TOP) as it captures every shadow, ornament, and blossom.

Lichens and moss (BOTTOM LEFT) cover a weathered boulder flanked by the deep reds of Japanese maple and barberry.

Dry-climate succulents send roots deep between stones (BOTTOM RIGHT). Despite the heat, foliage in shades of blue and gray imparts a frosty feeling.

A stone retaining wall creates a front-yard garden that hosts an assortment of perennials with varying forms and textures.

Getting to Know Stone

Throughout the pages of this book, you will see and learn ways to use stone and plants to transform your garden into a more artistic and enjoyable place. The plant palette available to you is nearly unlimited, but the situation is different with stone. If you live near a sizeable city, you will probably be able to locate a stoneyard where a wide array of stone is offered for sale. Yet many gardeners opt to follow a more personal path by collecting stone from land close to home. Whether you are planning to buy stone or gather your own, or trying to make up your mind, let me first arm you with some useful stone-related lingo to help you in procuring stone and putting it to its best use.

Rock vs. Stone

Technically, there is a big difference between rock and stone. Rock exists in a raw form, freshly broken or quarried from the earth, whereas stone is rock that has been exposed to the elements and subsequently smoothed, shaped, etched, or altered by wind, water, ice, and sun. Newly cut rock from a quarry *looks* new; at least five years pass before it appears weathered and well seasoned. Stone, on the other hand, has a visual character in keeping with the earth's surface, so it is widely preferred for use in gardens.

Natural stone is found in a number of places on or quite near the surface, often broken and weathered into the ideal sizes needed by stone-minded gardeners. Mountain streams offer up an endless supply of rounded stones, rocky hillsides often crumble into pieces, and the northern glaciers have left drifts of crushed and rounded stone in their wake. Where soil was rich in stone, Colonial American farmers often complained that they were growing more stone than food. No matter how many stones they picked out each year and piled into walls or dumped down ravines, there seemed to be even more the following spring. They were right, because after topsoil is loosened, freezing and thawing pushes a fresh crop of stones upward, just high enough to get in the way of a plow.

A good stoneyard is full of possibilities, such as rough stone you can pick through, or pallets loaded with preselected pieces.

Bringing Home the Stone

Just because good-looking stone exists in a certain place does not mean you can have it. First, you will need to be able to get to it with a truck, and if it's not your land, you will need permission to remove the stones you want. To many people, this is part of the thrill of the hunt; they enjoy finding and collecting stone as much as they like using it. After all, who would not love to have stone from a tumbled-down wall on an abandoned farm, or blocks from a 200-year-old chimney left standing decades after the house has perished? When seeking a landowner's consent to remove stone from his property to yours, be honest in your opinion that the stone is of value and offer to pay for it in cash, by the truckload. You will either be rewarded with an agreement to sell or be told that the stone is not for sale at any price. In this case, don't forget the final question: "Do you know of another place around here where I might get some stone like this?" Many beautiful garden scenes trimmed in stone began just this way.

Most of us end up buying stone at a stoneyard, where it is sold by the ton, usually stacked on pallets. Just as you might investigate natural stone by its look and feel, plan on taking the same approach at a stoneyard. Whether you are using found, recycled, or purchased stone, your projects will turn out better if you key your choice of stone to the way you want to use it in your garden. ■

Types of Stone

Every stone began as rock, and rocks vary in their color, density, and weight. Igneous rock, formed from the heat of volcanoes or from bubbling magma that cooled more slowly, is typically very hard and heavy. Except for granite and basalt, which I'll get to in a moment, igneous rocks are seldom used as the primary material in large garden building projects. Instead, various types of sedimentary rock, particularly limestone, sandstone, and shale, are the stones that are most often used to create walkways or walls, or to frame beds in a garden. Metamorphic rock, such as marble and slate, is as hard and heavy as igneous rock, despite the fact that marble began as limestone and slate began as shale — two comparatively soft sedimentary rocks.

Sedimentary stone, with its many layers, splits easily into flat pieces to make steps or resting places (LEFT).

Single-slab steps (ABOVE) are imaginatively cantilevered into a mortared wall at the Innisfree Garden in Millbrook, NY.

Sedimentary Rock

Sedimentary rock is great for building, because it naturally breaks into flat pieces. This tendency derives from the way sedimentary rock was formed, in layers, with a clearly discernible grain. Many types of sedimentary rock readily divide along the grain, like split wood, but splitting rocks successfully requires both practice and stone with a willing character.

Although we may shy away from projects that require splitting rocks, few of us get very far into gardening with stone before we end up staring at a piece that needs to be trimmed to fit where we want it to go. But even if you don't have to cut stone to fit, it's good to bang into a few just to see what's inside. As you will quickly discover, sedimentary rock is not only beautiful; it's infinitely interesting as well.

SOFT SANDSTONE. Anyone who has ever moved sheets of sandstone will bear witness that it is anything but lightweight. But compared with other types of stone, sandstone is surprisingly soft. It's easy to trim and easy to carve and can be cut to fit precisely against straight edges, such as those formed by the front steps of your house.

How can this be? As most gardeners know, sand is a large, coarse soil particle, compared with a clay particle, which is very small. Sandstone, comprised mostly of sand, includes interstices between the sand grains, and these tiny spaces are what give sandstone its light texture. Depending on the type of beach, lake, or desert that gave birth to the sandstone, it may be pink, tan, brown, orange, gray, or nearly white. Most brown-toned stone that you find sold as flagstone is sandstone.

Unfortunately, you cannot just go out wandering the hillsides and expect to find usable sandstone. If you do encounter sandstone in the wild, the first thing to do is to bang into it with a rock hammer to see if it shatters into a hundred pieces. Unless you live where better sandstones are common, expect found sandstone to be too soft, variable, and unstable for building.

You will doubtless find the best sandstone at a stoneyard, nicely split and ready to be trimmed to fit your new patio or walkway or to use as capstones for any type of wall. Naturally, small broken pieces are less costly than large sheets, and many a walkway has been created by combining large, comely flagstones with odd pieces of rubble. And, as you will see throughout this book, varying the color of stone in a garden floor has an arresting impact that can be every bit as appealing as sticking with a single color tone. Plus, you can always frame the edges of sandstone situated underfoot with some contrasting material, such as anything from plants to broken plates to upturned clay flowerpots.

Blocks of sandstone are infinitely carvable, though it's important when using carving tools to start slowly and carefully. You should take the time to get to know the strength of the specimen that you are tapping into before you launch into an

intricate design. Although sandstone is delicate and easily broken compared with harder types of stone, it is still so heavy that you will need crowbars, helpers, and perhaps a winch type of come-along to move large slabs from place to place.

Sandstone is easily shaped into blocks, often right at the quarry. A sandstone wall has a clean, tailored look.

Igneous Intensity

In the dead of winter, it's hard to accept that the planet upon which we live has at its core a bubbling ball of molten rock. But while our feet are freezing, somewhere else on the globe a huge steam vent is opening as the earth's interior literally boils open, releasing its pent-up heat through a volcano. When this happens and magma cools very quickly, the resulting rock may be riddled with open, bubblelike spaces as it spews through the air. Or, if it's inside the volcano itself, it may harden into extremely hard rock composed of tiny interlocking crystals — for example, glass-hard obsidian. Magma that cools at a slightly more moderate rate may harden into basalt, while pools of magma that are pushed near the surface remain so deep that they cool very slowly and frequently harden into granite.

Sometimes called "fire rock" because it is formed in conditions of extreme heat, igneous rock lacks the fissures and layering seen in sedimentary rocks, so it is not inclined to split easily into squared-off pieces. Instead, igneous rock must either be cut or be accepted as it is. Fortunately, there are many sites in which igneous rock is found already shattered and weathered into attractive pieces small enough for mere humans to handle.

GRAND GRANITE. Formed below the earth's surface over millions of years, granite has been pushed up to form mighty mountains. Granite varies in density, but it is always very hard, heavy, and liberally flecked with quartz crystals. Without heavy equipment, it is extremely difficult to cut or shape granite, both because of its hardness and because it usually lacks a discernible grain. When granite does crumble into pieces that are then exposed to the elements, the stones tend to be rounded in shape with few angular edges. Their roundness makes them difficult to stack, so mortar is often required to hold together stone walls made from granite.

You can buy granite that has been cut into pavers, flagstone, or building blocks, but even then, it is neither cheap nor particularly easy to handle. Recycled granite from old buildings is a true treasure, though difficult to find. In the interest of landscape unity, you may decide that granite is what you need if your

Hard, heavy granite is difficult to shape and to work with, but blocks of it provide a strong, ageless presence when used to build a garden wall.

A rugged garden in central California is tucked within a cluster of basalt boulders that opens to a broad vista featuring a lake.

yard already happens to be rich in granite boulders begging for company. In this case, you may want to use granite to edge a walkway or add visual interest and diversity to a limestone wall. Stoneyards often offer several types of cut or broken granite, which you will know by its weight and sparkle. Granite boulders are frequently sold, too, and they are so weighty that professional installation is usually required to make them a part of a garden.

BEAUTIFUL BASALT. The same processes that create granite cause the formation of basalt, which often has a columnar grain because it cools faster, often quite near areas where steam is moving along rivers of magma. Basalt is darker in color than granite, and harder, too, composed as it is from a mixture of very small crystals along with others that are medium to large. The western mountains offer up an assortment of basalts, including some very dark, fine-grained plateaus in Arizona and New Mexico, and slightly less dense deposits in the Pacific Northwest.

Like granite, basalt is typically tamed and shaped at the quarry to make it usable for flooring and building. However, if you live near where basalt occurs naturally, you may encounter special opportunities to use uncut pieces of basalt as specimen stones in your garden. Upright basalt pillars embody the energy of volcanoes, and their dark density always stands in stark contrast to plants with gray or variegated foliage.

CHAPTER 2

PATHWAYS WITH PURPOSE

We may take indoor floors for granted, but special surfaces underfoot outdoors often surprise us with their bold statements. As shelter for your feet, hard surfaces made of stone can't help but make a

garden feel more welcoming. Stepping-stones set in grass say "Come this way," and a stone patio splashed into a sunny spot of your yard says "Bask here." Outdoor floors and paths clearly define the places meant for people rather than plants, and they make your featured plantings more accessible and easier to enjoy.

A hedge of roses deserves an elegant pathway that invites people to linger among fragrant waist-high blossoms. Straight outside edges and closely fit stones give this walkway a nicely tailored look.

Walkways Up Front

A spacious expanse of stone just outside your front door breathes its beauty into everything around it and firmly connects your home to the solid earth. Whether you use it to widen a long walkway as it nears the entrance or to create a wide platform at the base of your front steps that feels like a welcoming patio, entryway stonework sets an elegant style that's easy to amplify with graceful plants. Large containers that coordinate with the colors of the stone can be

planted with splashy annuals, and you can use low-growing evergreens to add textural interest that will remain constant through the seasons.

Safety, comfort, and stability are top priorities for a front walkway, followed closely by curb appeal. A handsome front walkway enhances the value of your home while giving everyone who sees it a fleeting wave of pleasure. Front walkways, likely to be used by guests wearing their "good" shoes, need to be both smooth and wide. Walkways more than 3 feet wide are ideal, since they make it possible for two people to approach walking side by side. In northern areas, they need to be made in such a way that they can be kept clear of ice and snow in winter.

Smooth flagstone walkways create the clean, organized effect that we call formal, which is what people often want in their front yards. You will get the most formal look by using a single type of cut stone laid in a distinct pattern. The pattern may be subtle or very pronounced, depending on the look you want to achieve. There is no right or wrong way for you to do this, only endless creative opportunities, including the ones I'll describe here.

Plan in advance for some type of edge that will serve as a visual frame for your stonework. Neat, uniform plants such as liriope, candytuft, or ajuga are ideal, or you can use an evergreen ground cover such as English ivy or pachysandra.

If your home is brick, you can use brick to frame (or edge) your walkway, and possibly include brick

A wide, gently curving walkway with tightly fitted, flat stones offers a warm welcome and an opportunity to admire the colorful border.

in your stonework pattern as well. Both brick and stone can be dry-laid, but brick edgings stay put better when mortared into place. In fact, a mortared brick edging does an outstanding job of framing dry-laid stone.

An edging made of cut stone, laid on its side, also provides structural support. Or, if you want to evoke the feeling of a stream, you can arrange rounded stones around the edge of your walkway after it is finished, keeping in mind the way nature likes to tumble river rocks into scattered groups.

In the walkway itself, formal patterns often encompass a central line, or spine, made up of large stones that are sufficiently organized to impart a noticeable rhythm, flanked by a less disciplined pattern along the edges (see top right drawing below). In addition to looking handsomely refined, stone walkways structured this way are often more economical to build, because you can sink your money into pretty precut stones for the spine and use another less costly (or found) stone for the outer edges.

You can also pursue patterning differently, by using smaller stones in the center of the walkway and employing larger ones to establish a strong outline along the outer edges of the walk (see bottom right drawing below). This approach also is helpful where drainage is uncertain, because water that accumulates on the walkway can seep down through the many crevices between the small stones set in the middle.

Pathway Patterns

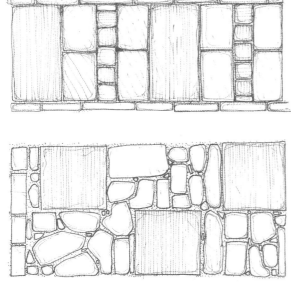

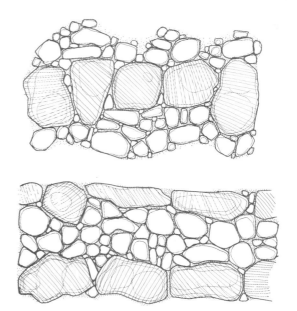

Purely geometric stones (TOP) convey formality; a juxtaposition of regular with irregular (BOTTOM) can be more intriguing.

Larger stones can provide a strong central spine (TOP) or can give greater definition to a path's edges (BOTTOM).

Making New Walkways

Before your heart becomes firmly set on a stone walk-way, you'll need to study exactly how walkways are built. Preparing the site often requires as much time and care as setting the stones, but it is not extremely difficult as long as you understand what you are doing. Of course, the degree of preparation depends on whether you are laying stones in turf or mortar or creating a dry-laid walkway. Because the latter approach is the one most often chosen by gardeners who want to make new walkways with their own hands, it is the one I will explain in detail. Also note that the same steps used to prepare a site for dry-laid stone apply to making gravel or pebble walkways capable of standing the test of time.

First I'll introduce you to the materials and what they do, and then we'll go through the installation process step by step. Study both the mental and the physical aspects of creating a walkway before you get started, and you can be assured of success.

Choosing Materials

Before you can budget your time and money, you'll need to weigh the pros and cons of different materials. The first decision, of course, is choosing the paving material itself. Paving stones that are more than 3 inches thick, such as flat pieces of fieldstone, are heavy to handle, but because of their weight, they hold their position very well. This means the foundation beneath the walkway does not need to be as deep as if you were using 2-inch-thick pieces of flagstone. After choosing your paving material, measure its thickness, because this factor influences both the depth of the foundation and what you will use to fill the crevices between the stones.

A narrow pathway made of thick, heavy stepping-stones assures safe footing through a shady sea of ground covers toward a quiet pool.

Foundation Factors

In any climate, using any type of paving stone, you will need to excavate a foundation for your walkway. The foundation is filled from the bottom up with a layer of fine gravel, then a layer of paver base (also known as crushed rock — see the box below for the different terms used for these materials), and finally your paving stone of choice. The purpose of the foundation is threefold: It aids in drainage; provides a bed for the stone; and, in cold regions, expands and contracts when the surrounding soil freezes and thaws, reducing the likelihood that your paving stones will sink down or pop up in response to changes in the weather.

In climates where soil freezes more than 6 inches deep, the foundation needs to be 12 inches below the surface. After excavating the site to this depth, measure the thickness of your paving stone and add 2 inches (the depth of the middle layer of paver base) to that number. Subtract the total thickness of these two layers from 12 inches, and you will know how deep a layer of fine gravel you need to place in the excavated site.

In climates where the soil seldom freezes, or freezes only 4 inches down, the foundation need not be as deep. However, you still need the enhanced drainage from the gravel base and the excellent seating you get from the middle layer of paver base. In USDA Hardiness Zones 7 to 10 (see map, page 232), a base layer of 2 inches of gravel is sufficient. This means that if you are using 2-inch-thick stone, you will need to excavate only 6 inches deep — 2 inches for the gravel, 2 inches for the paver base, and 2 inches for the stone.

Paver Base and Processed Gravel

Paver base (middle layer) is rock dust or crushed rock, which some stonemasons call fines or crushing dust. This is the same material used to make foundations for concrete landscaping blocks, so it is sold by all home supply stores that sell landscaping blocks. Some landscapers use coarse sand in its place, but paver base, made of tiny rock shards mixed with fine rock dust, packs down beautifully and is not as likely to shift as sand. Paver base is usually sold in 50-pound bags; each contains one-half cubic foot. Packed 2 inches deep, one bag covers only 3 square feet. If you have a lot of ground to cover, it is more economical to buy paver base by the ton from a sand and gravel supplier. At 2 inches deep, a ton of paver base covers about 120 square feet.

Processed gravel (bottom layer) is finer than the gravel used on unpaved roads; pieces should be about ¾ inch in diameter. Fine pea gravel works, too, though it does not pack as firmly as processed gravel. Unless your project is very small, buy this material in bulk. The weight is about the same as that of paver base:

1 ton of processed gravel covers 120 square feet about 2 inches deep. So if you need 6 inches of processed gravel, you will need 3 tons to cover 120 square feet. It's very easy to underestimate how much paver base or crushed gravel a walkway requires, so my advice is to be on the safe side and buy extra. ■

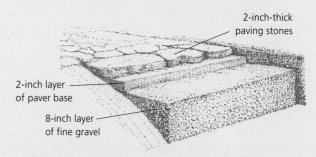

A deep bed of processed gravel topped by paver base forms a good walkway foundation.

Preventing Drainage Disasters

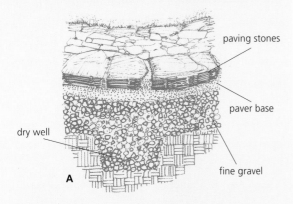

paving stones

paver base

dry well

fine gravel

A

A properly constructed dry-laid walkway will improve drainage problems rather than make them worse, because water will simply filter through the crevices and into the gravel bed below. If you are making a walkway in a flood-prone site, however, it may be wise to install a dry well at the lowest point. A dry well is basically a hole filled with gravel where water can collect and slowly disperse (A).

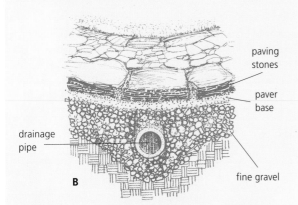

paving stones

paver base

drainage pipe

fine gravel

B

Alternatively, you can lay gravel-covered perforated drainage pipe under the walkway in places where water from your house or gutters is likely to run (B). Install this special drainage feature when you excavate the bed and before you fill it with the foundation materials.

Filling Crevices, Finishing Edges

In addition to paving stone, paver base, and processed gravel, you will need material to fill the joints. Either paver base or processed gravel can be used. Processed gravel is fine for filling crevices between thick stones, and one advantage to using gravel is that it doesn't stick to the bottom of your shoes, so it makes a cleaner walking surface. Paver base, which is finer, works best with thin flagstones or small cobbles. Rain and regular sweeping will often keep the paver base sufficiently recessed in the crevices so that the walkway stays reasonably clean. Because paving stone is always set directly into a bed of paver base, some paver base will inevitably show between the crevices that are filled with gravel. However, when it is mixed with packed processed gravel, the paver base will usually fade from view.

A properly excavated and installed stone walkway needs no edging material, but if you want edging for aesthetic purposes, it's best to install it before the stone is laid. For example, if you want to outline your walkway with brick or wood, get the edging situated over the foundation before you begin placing stones.

You may also be pondering which plants you might use to fill large pockets along the edges, or perhaps you are considering a second type of stone (such as rounded river stone) for covering pockets where you choose not to place plants. Wait until after your walkway is complete to set out plants or purely decorative stone edgings.

Planting Your Walkway

In a shady garden walkway, crevices that can support plants or moss are highly desirable. If the walkway receives more sun than the surrounding spaces, you won't want to miss the opportunity to grow plants in the crevices. At first, many of those plants will be weeds that you will have to pull, but over time you will find more attractive plants with the tenacity to hold on to their space, thus limiting the growth of weeds. For some choices, see "Comely Plants for Crevices" on pages 74 to 77. Of course, you might also make friends with certain weeds that make acceptable crevice plants, such as wild violets, cinquefoil, or wood sorrel.

As for the edging plants, plan ahead to include occasional upright plants that appear to have moved into the pathway on their own. For example, if drifts of columbine, blue phlox, foxglove, stachys, or shade-loving cranesbills grow near the path, plant a matching specimen or two in a pocket along the edge. Similarly, you can create small outcroppings of piled or planted stones that reach out into the garden to help exemplify the natural tension that exists between the human presence (the path) and the reigning power of the woods of which the path is a part.

Get Creative in Crevices

The spaces between the stones in a walkway or patio can be narrow or quite wide, depending on the effect you want to achieve. Thin crevices filled with leached, acidic soil or peat moss will eventually support soft green moss if they are kept sufficiently damp. Broader crevices filled with light-colored gravel make the walkway easier to see after dark and give better traction in wet weather.

Use a small metal rod (a 12-inch-long rebar stake works well) to firmly pack the crevices between stones with gravel or sand when you first set the stones in place. Leave the crevices slightly recessed if you wish to fill them with the mulch, such as finely shredded bark, that you are using in nearby sections of your garden. If you want to encourage low-growing plants, such as herbs or sedums, fill large crevices with a rich mixture of compost, sand, and native soil. ◼

An irresistible pondside oasis made of light-colored flagstone is actually two patios connected by a walkway.

Lay Down a Weed Barrier

If you wish, you can spread landscaping fabric over the walkway base to serve as a barrier against deeply rooted weeds. This is particularly wise if you are laying stones in soil or in a shallow bed (as is done with gravel walkways). In more deeply prepared beds, most of the weeds that appear between crevices don't emerge from under the stones but sprout from windblown seeds that lodge themselves in the cracks. ■

Digging In

Now let's assume that you understand your options in terms of design and materials and you're ready to get to work on your new walkway. You may have a detailed plan, which is good, but as you'll see, it's important to be ready to revise it as needed once you start actually creating a walkway of stone.

Begin by marking and measuring the space where you want your new walkway to go. Use wood stakes and string for straight walkways. For curved ones, lay garden hoses or lengths of rope over the ground to experiment with preliminary perimeters. Take some time with this step, spending a few days playing with different possibilities for the layout and walking within the boundaries you've set up.

Trimming Flagstone

When you're working with flagstone and you can't find a piece that's exactly the right size for a certain spot, you may need to trim it to fit. However, to get a straight edge, you cannot count on a solid whack from a heavy hammer to do the job right. Because most flagstone is layered sedimentary rock, without some direction on your part, it will likely shatter into jagged pieces. In order to control the cut, you will first need to score a ¼-inch-deep groove along the cutting line before knocking off the excess.

Many professional stonemasons use a double-insulated circular saw with an abrasive masonry blade to score cutting lines in flagstone, and you can use this method, too. If you have only a few stones to trim, you can do pretty well with a cold chisel and a heavy stone hammer. Mark the cutting line (A), then use the chisel to score it (B). When the groove is ¼ inch deep, place the stone on the ground with a board under it. The idea is to have the body of the stone very well supported, so that when you strike the tag end with as much force as you can muster, it will break away in precisely the right place. Practice on unremarkable pieces before trimming stones that you have picked out as personal favorites.

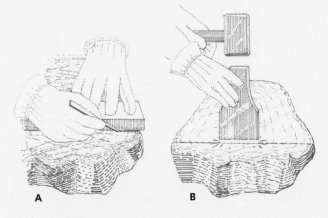

A   B

NOTE: Whenever you are cutting into stone, you *must* protect your eyes with safety goggles.

As you position your new walkway, be sure to investigate grade — the degree to which the surface is sloped. For good drainage, a walkway (or any paved surface) should have a very slight slope. Be sure the slope is away from your house, so that you aren't directing water runoff right to your foundation. You can alter the grade slightly as you excavate the site and lay down the gravel bed. If you are confronted by a pronounced slope in the wrong direction, you'll need to make a radical change and design your entire walkway around the drainage problem, rather than expect to fix it by covering it up with stone. (See "Preventing Drainage Disasters" on page 50 for ways to work walkways into flood-prone sites.)

A Walkway Walk-Through

Dig the Foundation Bed

Digging out the soil is the biggest part of laying a walk, and it should be done by hand using a shovel and a wheelbarrow. Plan ahead for where you will put all that excavated soil, for it will quickly grow into a small mountain. As you excavate, use a carpenter's level to check the grade across the walkway. From high side to low side, a slope of about ⅛ inch per foot is ideal. If you need to, you can use some of your excavated soil to raise the high side to achieve a proper crosswise grade.

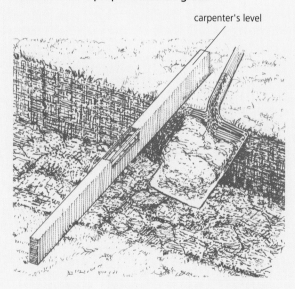

carpenter's level

Add and Tamp the Gravel

Fill the excavated site with the amount of processed gravel you have estimated you will need. Dump an approximate amount into the entire walkway, use a shovel and rake to distribute it evenly, and then start at one end tamping the gravel into place with a tamping tool. You can buy a metal tamping tool or make one by nailing a flat piece of wood onto a wood handle. After tamping a few square feet, use a yardstick or a ruler to

measure the tamped depth. If the level is too low, add more gravel before tamping the rest. Tamping gets tiresome quickly, and you don't want to have to do it twice.

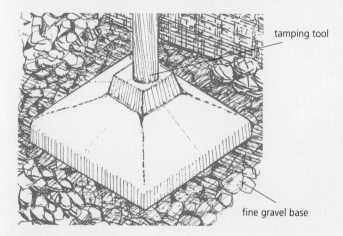

tamping tool

fine gravel base

Add the Paver Base

Use a wheelbarrow or a shovel to gently dump paver base onto the tamped processed gravel. Rake it out evenly, and then do some preliminary tamping to make sure you have a good 2-inch-thick base. When you're satisfied with its depth, tamp it well and then dampen it thoroughly before going back and tamping again.

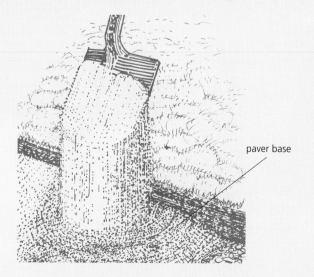

paver base

Position the Stones

After all the work of bed preparation, the slow process of arranging stones is a welcome change. While there are practical matters to consider, the artistry of the task is equally important, and it can be deeply satisfying, too. Set your own pace, and don't be reluctant to redo sections that fall short in terms of fit or flow.

Begin by picking through your pile of stone, selecting pieces that have straight edges. These can be used for the outside edges of your walkway without having to be trimmed first. The less trimming you must do, the better. If your site includes any corners or other right angles, look for stone that already shows this shape. Because corners or other defined angles are the hardest ones to fit, select stones for those areas first and set them in place. Naturally, the flattest side of any stone is the side that should be placed facing up.

As you pick through your pile, set aside small stones that are extra thick, or those that appear unusable unless they are placed on their sides so that they dagger down into the bed. These are exactly the stones you will need to fill in small gaps between larger stones. Small stones need to be set deeply to keep them from popping out.

Begin laying the stones in the foundation bed, starting at the most well-defined corner or straight edge. You don't have to lay down the whole walkway before actually setting the stones in place, but it is nice to have a solid idea of any pattern you see emerging or of the exact placement of especially attractive stones. Throw pieces of scrap plywood down on the places yet to be filled with stone, so that you can walk on the plywood without disturbing the foundation.

Set the Stones

Remove the stones from the bed, a few at a time, and set them aside. They will be easier to move back into place if you keep them on their sides and lean them against something solid. Now you're ready to begin permanently installing each stone in the walkway.

During this process, your most important tool is a carpenter's level, which you will use constantly as you nestle individual stones into the foundation bed. Use gloved hands and a small trowel to add or subtract rock dust as needed to make sure each stone is at precisely the right height. Work in tiers across the walkway, stopping after each tier to check both the level of each stone and the pitch of the walkway. Correct any bulges or dips before going on to the next tier.

Filling Crevices

Although you don't have to stop to fill crevices after laying each tier of stones, don't get too far into your walkway before pausing to pack crevices with rock dust. And I do mean pack. It is not sufficient to simply sweep rock dust into the crevices unless they are so close and tight that you can't poke the filler in with a metal rod. The point of actually poking filler into the joints is to force it into the small pockets beneath the edges of the stones, further anchoring them into place.

It helps to stand or kneel on the stones as you work the crevices, rocking your weight a little to test for any loose spots where the stones may not be well supported by the bed. Stop to fix these trouble spots as soon as you find them. If you can't work enough rock dust under the stone by packing it into the closest crevice, you may need to use a pry bar to lift the edge of the stone and add or subtract rock dust to get it set rock solid in its place.

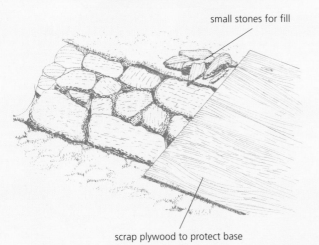

small stones for fill

scrap plywood to protect base

Linking the Landscape

If you think of walkways as invitations, you may be inspired to use stone to direct footsteps to parts of your landscape that deserve to be visited easily and often. Invariably, a path to a backyard garden passes through a side yard, which can become a beautiful garden spot in its own right when it is brought into sharp focus by a stone walkway. Because side yards are often shady and narrow, they naturally lend themselves to landscaping approaches that emphasize coziness and secrecy. So, rather than a wide, formal walkway, a series of rustic stepping-stones set in soil and surrounded by mulch or small plants may be most appropriate where the primary point is simply to enjoy the journey.

Depending on what you want a walkway to do, it can be short or long, curved or straight, intermittent or continuous. The main thing to keep in mind is that any type of walkway — no matter where it's situated — always has something to say. It is never silent, because its purpose is to show people how to get from one place to another. Your task is to use stone creatively to make your walkways speak in a language easily understood by everyone.

A stone pathway that leads to or winds through a garden is very much a part of the garden itself. Here we will look at informal stone pathways for gardens that receive partial shade. Sunnier sites that can support grass get their turn in a few pages.

A Path Through Nature

Informal stone pathways in lush wooded sites tell several stories. In addition to the obvious one — that this is a passageway that leads somewhere — surrounding plants suggest nature's inexorable desire to reclaim the pathway as its own. Small plants may creep in from the edges, and foliage from nearby shrubs may trickle into the opening created by the walkway. One particularly effective way to dramatize this story is to conjure up a feeling of enclosure by locating small trees or lean, upright shrubs a few feet outside the pathway. Because the opening for the pathway receives more light than the rest of the area, plants quite naturally lean in toward the path to take advantage of the light. Vine-covered arches or overhead limbs sculpted into bowers add another dimension that deepens the mystique of a woodland walkway.

With the plants pressing in on the pathway and thus creating a feeling of natural force, the stone placement should show clear organization and rhythm to further help the path stand out. It should communicate the idea that people are as welcome in this place as the plants that are the true hosts.

You can use different types of stone, as long as their placement clearly shows how they are related. For instance, whether you use small cobblestones, rounded limestone from streambeds, or flat pieces of flagstone, lay the largest stones along the outside edges of the path, with smaller stones toward the center, to create a scene reminiscent of a well-trodden path in the woods. At first glance, it's not hard to imagine how years of use might have cracked and pounded the middle of the path, altering its texture.

Flatter is usually better when it comes to paving stone, but if your garden path climbs a slight slope into the woods, a rough walking surface can be an advantage. Besides increasing traction, it won't be as slick when glazed with ice. A serious slope calls for steps, but modest inclines paved with rough stone often have a tranquil, dreamlike quality.

An informal corridor through a side yard is dramatically lit by shafts of sunlight shining through openings in the foliage.

Backyard Basics

As our landscapes develop, we often find that our backyards gradually evolve into a cluster of outdoor rooms, each with its special purpose — an eating area, a sunning spot, and, of course, different types of gardens. By making small shifts in the pattern of stonework or the color and texture of the stones used for walkways, you can signal the transition from one "room" to another. For example, you might use a series of broad, flat stepping-stones nestled into your lawn to link your deck or patio to a shade garden beneath a stately tree. Then, to accentuate the garden threshold, you could create a unique stone pattern, such as a mosaic flooring of small, rounded cobblestones, that opens into the intimate sitting area beneath the branches.

Indeed, the only rules for creating stone pathways in your backyard is that they help you garden better, make sense to visitors, and don't overpower the plants for which they are meant to be gentle company. Changes in color and pattern give subtle cues about transitions and help make a backyard more interesting and mysterious.

In the backyard, even the width of walkways is a bit of a wild card. As gardeners, we often become so enthralled with plants — and surprised by their exuberance when they are bursting with health — that we are willing to keep paths only wide enough to shimmy through, our thighs brushed with foliage as we pass. Narrow pathways are always intimate, but they can be somewhat foreboding as well. Very

Rounded river stones, set on edge, form a well-defined pathway through a garden lush with annuals, including sanvitalia, runner beans, and towering white cleome. When the planting plan changes, so can the walkway.

Strategically set in a lawn, a cluster of stepping-stones at the end of a path almost magnetically carries the visitor to the best place for viewing the garden, and also saves wear and tear on the turf.

narrow walkways require a bit of concentration to negotiate, so they're not as restful as wider paths. You can play with these differences by having wide sections give way to narrower side paths or detours, which are often needed to access remote areas of the garden. Don't forget to take into account practical considerations, such as places in the garden where pathways need to be wide enough to accommodate a wheelbarrow. Even if your inclination is to have a backyard that's jungle-thick with plants, you will need to provide some reassuringly wide areas here and there, which you can create easily enough with oases of stone.

Stepping into a Small Lawn

If you have a lovely small lawn and want to improve access to it, you may need a threshold more than you need an actual pathway. The place where you first step into the lawn is the logical place, because that is where grass often becomes compacted and thin from too many footfalls. A closely spaced grouping of flat stones solves the problem, while giving people a place to pause as they decide what to do next. Should you take off your shoes and let the turf tingle between your toes, lie in it and gaze at the sky, or simply stand and breathe it in? An artful landing says exactly what needs to be said: "Come in, pause, and linger."

The irregular pattern of the flush-laid paving stones is accentuated by the brilliant green ground cover of Corsican mint.

Splendor in the Grass

Clipped grass keeps you busy in the summertime, but it pays you back with several wonderful attributes — a neat, formal appearance, a feeling of spaciousness, textural contrast with plants and hard surfaces, and a place to romp or relax. A lawn's visual appeal lies in its carpetlike expanse, which is radically interrupted by a stepping-stone walkway. Preserving the expansive aura of your lawn while facilitating foot traffic with stone is a challenge loaded with paradox.

Two tips may be helpful. The first is to leave as much grassy space as is comfortable between stepping-stones, so that the lawn retains its position at center stage. Keep in mind that spacing helps set the pace, too. Stones set close together in a straight line encourage fast walking, while people move more slowly across widely spaced stones that meander a bit. The second strategy is to include another landscape feature, such as a line of shrubs, a low stone wall, or a clearly outlined flower bed that creates a pull toward the stone pathway, continuing or echoing the line it makes in the landscape. This design approach makes the walkway appear to flow through the landscape rather than breaking it into pieces.

One of the nifty things about installing a stone pathway in turf is that you can experiment endlessly with possible layouts by simply placing the stones on the lawn where you think you may want them to go. You can try out a single straight line or make it double wide, switch to a gentle curve, or even zigzag a little if you have other landscape features that are best accessed in this way. If the pathway links two clear destinations, such as a patio and a water garden, you may want to cluster several stepping-stones at the approach to each — a way of letting your feet know that they have arrived someplace special.

Installing Stone in Turf

The simplest way to install stepping-stones in turf is first to position a stone and cut around it with the end of a sharp spade, cookie-cutter style (A).

A

Next, flip over the stone and remove the sheet of turf along with the soil beneath it (B). Use a ruler or measuring tape to dig precisely to the thickness of the stone plus 1 inch, keeping the bottom of the hole flat and compacted.

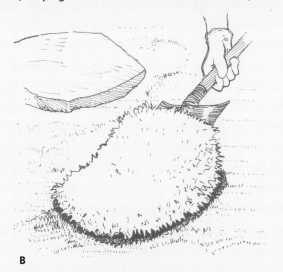

B

Fill the bottom with 1 inch of sand (C), dampen it lightly, replace the stone, and then stand on it and do the "Twist" for a few seconds. Your gyrations will help settle the stone in place.

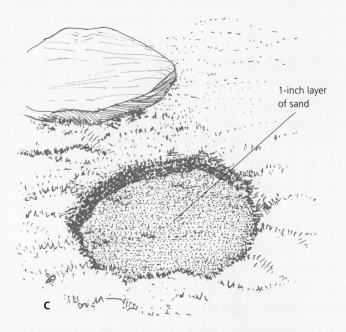

1-inch layer of sand

C

A perfectly set stone will sit ¼ inch above surrounding soil, so that after a few weeks it will settle to be flush with the surface. When stones are set at this level, you can mow right over them even when clipping your lawn very low.

Some stones may need slight adjustments, particularly if their bottom sides have bumps or ridges. If the stone wobbles when you dance on it, use a pry bar to lift the unstable side and add (or subtract) sand as needed to get the stone firmly seated in place. Give very odd-shaped stones extra support by using small rocks as shims. Wiggle the shims down into the sand, set the stone in place, and then make adjustments with more shims and sand, if needed. You may also need to pack small amounts of sand into the crevices around the outside of the stone to limit shifting and possible problems with fast-growing weeds.

A pattern of interlocking stepping-stones within a bed of pebbles mimics footprints and urges you down the path toward a striking millstone feature.

Embedded Stepping-Stones

A stone pathway does not have to be comprised exclusively of large stones. Although flat, heavy stepping-stones provide solid stability, you may prefer to set large stones into a bed of smaller ones, such as pea gravel, small rounded river stones, or a mixture. Alternatively, you may use finely shredded bark or wood chips, well tamped so they don't wash away. When you use mixed materials, just be sure to keep in mind how one material relates to another and how the finished composition fits into the site while doing the job for which it is intended.

CHOOSING MATERIALS. The largest stones you use will give strong focus to the shape and direction of the path, so give careful thought to their placement. Rustic stepping-stones set apart suggest slow movement, for instance. You can cluster stones together to signal pivot points, such as a place where a new pathway branches off or a spot that deserves a pause for a closer look. It's a good idea to lay out a few yards of feature stones before you begin preparing the site. Besides inspiring your work, this rough draft will show you how the walkway you have pictured in your mind will look when it is finished.

GRAVEL BASE. Walkways made with stepping-stones surrounded by gravel have much greater stability than plain gravel walkways, which invariably shift about underfoot. However, the deeper the gravel, the more you may feel like you're sinking into it if you step onto the gravel rather than the stepping-stones. Walking in more than 2 inches of loose gravel can feel like walking in soup. For these reasons, you'll need to prepare the site to provide for a firm 2-inch layer of gravel on a 1-inch layer of sand or rock dust. Assuming your stepping-stones are about 2 inches thick, this means excavating the entire site to a depth of 3 inches. For thicker and more irregular stepping-stones, you will need to custom-fit each in place before preparing the surrounding areas for gravel.

WEED CONTROL. Because weeds often appear in pebble walkways, it's best to line the excavated site with landscape fabric. Most weeds are annuals that actually seed in from above rather than creep in from beneath, but those that do grow from below — nutsedge, bermuda, and quack grass, for example — will ruin a loose walkway in a hurry. If you lay out the landscape fabric before you install the edging (see below), the edging will help secure the edges of the fabric, limiting its tendency to shift out of place.

Pull out weeds while they're young, before their roots have penetrated the landscape fabric. Some people use herbicides to keep their pebble walkways free from weeds. If you use chemical weed controls, be extremely careful to keep from injuring nearby plants. Use herbicides only in warm, still weather, and spot-treat weeds rather than spray large areas.

EDGING MATTERS. After excavating the site and laying the landscape fabric, install some type of edging that will keep the gravel in place. You can use treated lumber, plastic or metal edging, or brick, or you can make an edging of cut stones.

INSTALLING THE STONES. A 1-inch foundation of firmly packed sand or paver base, spread over the landscape fabric and then dampened and tamped, makes a fine bed for gravel or small river stones, as well as larger stepping-stones. This type of walkway moves as the ground heaves, which is why it is acceptable to use sand here. When the foundation layer is in place, install your largest stones first, using a level to make sure they are set at exactly the right height relative to one another. You may need to add more sand or crushed rock to get the big stepping-stones level and even. Then move on to smaller cobblestones if you wish to use them to create a pattern. Add the gravel last, firmly tamping it in place around the larger stones.

Cobblestone Pads

If you have an unlimited supply of small cobblestones, broken rock pieces, or pretty river stones, consider mortaring them together into stepping-stone–sized pads surrounded by pebble mulch. After preparing the site with landscape fabric and a bed of sand or crushed rock, build two or three wooden forms for the pads. Each form should be the size of one or two pads. Lay them in place and fill them one at a time with 1 to 3 inches of wet mortar. Push your selected stones into the mortar until they are embedded to two-thirds their thickness and the tops are level. Spray lightly with water and wipe up any spilled mortar. Then go on to the next pad, which will give the first one the hour or so it needs to set. You can then gently pry up the form from the first pad and use it to frame pad number three. Wait several days before filling in between the pads with gravel, and do not walk on the pads for at least a week. Although mortar appears dry after a few days, it becomes much harder over time.

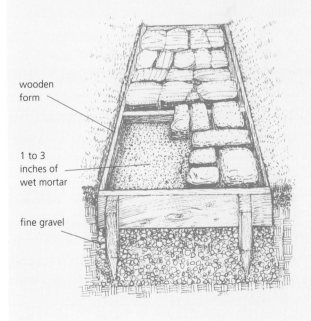

wooden form

1 to 3 inches of wet mortar

fine gravel

Like islands in a shallow sea, widely spaced stepping-stones meander through the gravel portion of a Japanese garden.

Malleable Gravel

Many people are so deeply pleased by a feeling of open space that they make an expanse of gravel or pebbles the centerpiece of their gardens. At first glance, this seems to be a very austere approach to gardening, but upon closer examination, it is rich with mysterious possibilities. Each plant that is situated in or near a gravel garden gains unmatched clarity for its texture and form, as do larger stones and stepping-stones that are planted in the sea of gravel.

In addition to your personal taste and vision for your garden — which might be in the style of a Southwestern desert, a Japanese rock garden, or a beach complete with driftwood — the suitability of the site will determine your success with an expanse of combed gravel. Ideally, the site will be nearly level, with only enough slope for sufficient drainage, and there will be some convenient vantage point, such as

a raised deck or patio, for viewing the garden from above. Sun or shade is unimportant, though open sites that are naturally free from excessive plant debris are much easier to maintain than those that are constantly being bombarded with leaves and twigs from overhanging trees. It's imperative to clean these away, because besides looking unkempt, plant debris that falls into gravel slowly accumulates as organic matter, which in time can give rise to numerous unwanted weeds. And, unfortunately, once a good supply of dirt gets into gravel, it is impossible to get it out.

Gravel gardens always include accent stones or plants, arranged so that the way they relate to one another — and to the gravel that surrounds them — suggests a feeling of floating islands. From both aesthetic and practical viewpoints, it's best to decide on the position of these islands at the same time that you define the edges of the gravel garden. Indeed, you should "plant" boulders, specimen stones, and shrubs or trees before you prepare the site for gravel, so you won't risk getting soil in otherwise clean gravel. See page 206 for tips on setting large boulders in place.

You will also need some kind of edging that does not interfere with the level plane that is so heavily accentuated by a gravel garden. Cut stone laid end to end is ideal. Or, if the gravel garden adjoins a section of lawn, you could use light-colored pavers that also serve as a mowing strip.

Installing a gravel garden is similar to making a gravel walkway. After you have set your large accent stones or plants, excavate the remaining area to a depth of 3 inches, install a sheet of landscaping fabric and an edging, and then fill with 1 inch of tamped damp sand. Landing stones or flat stepping-stones should be installed at this point, and it's best to keep them few and far between to keep from interrupting the flow of the space.

Finding just the right gravel for filling the garden may require some careful shopping. Very fine, well-rinsed pea gravel will work, but you may prefer to use finely crushed marble or granite because of their even color and clean appearance. If you want to rake patterns into the gravel in the tradition of Zen gardens, choose poultry grit, which many gardeners have found is just the right consistency for sculpted raking. You can buy poultry grit at farm supply stores in 50- and 100-pound bags.

Gravel gardens that are kept reasonably clean and regularly raked usually have few problems with weeds, because the raking process dislodges small seedlings while they are young and vulnerable. Limiting water also deters weeds, and it's a happy coincidence that a good cover of gravel insulates plant roots so well that shrubs and small trees growing in a gravel garden seldom require supplemental water.

Accents Underfoot

A gravel garden is intended to be experienced by the mind more than by the feet, but that does not mean that you must always be content to linger at its edges. Large, flat threshold stones set just inside the most approachable edge can help mark the garden's beginning, and from there a series of rounded stepping-stones might lead inward or disappear behind a larger stone or shrub. However, it's important always to keep in mind that the empty spaces of a gravel garden are not empty at all but hold just as much energy as more tangible rocks and plants. And if you add the element of movement by raking ripple-like patterns into the gravel, it becomes even more crucial that stepping-stones give the illusion that they are floating, as if on water.

Raking Ripples

A gravel-filled, framed panel that will be raked into patterns is one garden situation where you must definitely begin with the end in mind. Where will you stand as you rake? If you can stand only outside the gravel, your ability to mold curves or circles will be seriously limited. For this reason, it's often wise to strategically place one or more large, flat stones within the gravel garden. Besides providing structure and contrast, the stones provide a place to stand while you wield your rake, a job that requires good strength and balance. Japanese gardeners use special, very heavy rakes with long tines to rake patterns into gravel, but in a small garden, you can do a good job with a metal rake with sturdy prongs or a long-handled cultivator called a pronged hoe. ■

Patterned Mosaics

Perhaps the most ancient form of decorating a floor, mosaics made from stones laid in patterns have been found in archaeological sites dating back to the fifth century B.C. Historians believe that the first artists to create mosaics from pebbles were the Greeks. Eventually, craftsmen learned to cut and polish stones into tiny tiles, which simplified the creation of detailed pictures in mosaic. Renaissance artists elevated mosaic to a high art, as in the pristine creations preserved in St. Peter's Basilica in Rome. Simple mosaic patterns in stone are enjoying a revival in modern gardens because they are both impressively beautiful and easy to create. By using stones of varying colors, sizes, and textures, arranged in a dramatic or pleasing pattern, you can create a stone mosaic of any size for any site. And, because the stones used in a mosaic are small, you can often collect most of your materials from natural places, making your creation even more original and meaningful.

When envisioning a stone mosaic for your garden's floor, think of it as a work of art that will stand alone. Contrast between the colors and textures of the stones you choose will give your design strong impact, as will incorporating a sense of movement into the design. One of the oldest trends in mosaic design, *opus vermiculatum,* uses strong curves or circles. The name translates as "wormlike" — a fine theme to keep in mind as you dream up patterns for your one-of-a-kind garden mosaic.

You can frame your mosaic with grass, stone, or pavers to set it off as a prominent landscape feature, or let it grow right in the midst of the garden, sure to delight all who discover it resting among flowers and foliage. Whether framed or left to float in the garden, a mosaic of small stones and cobbles works like an Oriental rug, bringing an element of liveliness to an otherwise quiet outdoor scene.

If your garden vision involves paving a long walkway in a swirling mosaic pattern, keep the design simple and repetitive. In fact, you will probably find that it is more effective (and more fun) to create a circular or half-moon mosaic of stones at a stopping place or sitting area, where the design can be slowly savored up close.

Although you may feature a few large, flat stones in your design, the most interesting mosaics are made from small, smooth stones, such as river stones. Whether you collect or buy them, do not underestimate how many stones you will need; they often number in the thousands when you are placing small stones close together. Take the time to sort them into buckets according to shape and color. As you sort, pause from time to time to consider possible combinations and patterns that seem promising. For example, although you might initially plan to weave a mosaic from bands of gray, brown, and black stones of varying shapes, including some stark white stones or ruddy orange ones in your pattern may give the composition an extra surge of contrast that magically brings it to life.

Patterns with thick stones can be set in a 2-inch bed of paver base, but set small stones in a bed of wet cement. Or create unique mosaics in concrete stepping-stones, made in small wood frames with corners you can unscrew once the cement has set.

Eclectic stones, pebbles, plants, and concrete stepping-stones embedded with flat river rock contribute color, texture, and one-of-a-kind style to this mosaic walkway.

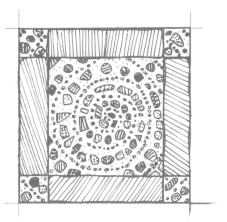

A radial pattern of multicolored stones is an easy and fun first-time mosaic project.

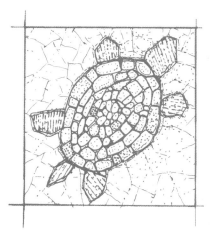

Motifs such as fish and turtles are suitable subjects for stone mosaics near water features.

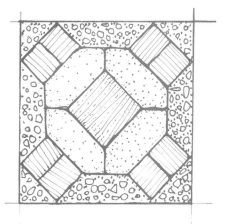

Scrap pieces of sandstone flags can be trimmed to form formal, geometric mosaics.

Composing a Mosaic

Making an outdoor floor in a mosaic pattern is a slow, organic process that cannot be done overnight. Besides, rushing through the job shortcuts the pure pleasure of this incredibly creative process. As you work, you may think of plant pairings or other adornments, such as containers or rock statuary, that belong in the picture. Instead of dismissing these ideas as distractions, incorporate them into the scene as it emerges. For example, a curve of stones along the edge may be just right for framing a stone water bowl, or you may discover places where your mosaic design deserves to be interrupted by a favorite plant.

Site preparation for an informal mosaic can be as simple as removing existing vegetation and lining the area with an inch or two of coarse sand. In shady sites, mixing the sand with one-third part peat moss will encourage the growth of moss between the stones. Mosaic work sets a proper mood for surprises, so offbeat accents such as half-buried blue bottles or sheet-metal dragonflies are welcome.

Whenever you are working with small stones, it is crucial to place them very close together. It also helps to structure your design so that it includes some flat stones set on their ends, to stabilize the placement of smaller stones set nearby. You will also need to keep a carpenter's level handy to check often for high spots and dips. A walkway or landing comprised of small stones will always be a little uneven, but it must be flat enough to foster safe footing and not so bumpy that it is impossible to sweep clean.

STONE SKILLS ■ ■ ■ ■

A Place to Work

Creating a mosaic of cobbles, river stones, and pebbles requires several sessions, so plan ahead to protect the prepared site from heavy deluges and unavoidable foot traffic. The easiest way is to cover your work in progress with a large piece of scrap plywood or a tarp. When you settle in to work, pull the plywood away a short distance and use it as a place to sit or kneel while you carefully place your stones. You can also use it as a place to keep stones within easy reach, along with hand tools, including a level and a small mason's hammer — the perfect tool for digging small trenches for unusually long stones set among smaller specimens.

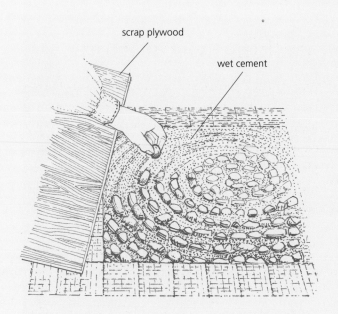

scrap plywood

wet cement

In many outdoor labyrinths, the center is marked by a flat stone for sitting or, as seen here, by an upright touchstone.

Walking Meditation

Any garden is the scene of a certain amount of meditation. We have quiet conversations with ourselves as we pull weeds or groom flowers, and many people create special corners for solitude in their gardens — places where they can be still and enjoy a break from the hurry and noise of the outside world, surrounded by the beauty of nature.

A labyrinth is just this sort of special space. It fosters meditation as you walk a coiled path that leads to the center and back out again, a metaphor for our journey through life. People who use labyrinths describe experiences similar to those encountered in other types of meditation — enhanced contact with their inner selves, strengthening of faith, and renewal of spiritual energy.

Labyrinths are often thought of as inventions of early Christians, but they have been around for more than 4,000 years. Their designs can be found in Hopi medicine wheels, Celtic circles, and symbols from many other cultures. Today some churches use canvas labyrinths to help people rediscover the magic of *solvitur ambulato,* meaning "it is solved by walking." Outdoor labyrinths, structured in stone and enriched with beautiful and fragrant plants, turn a garden into a sacred place that enriches the soul and the earthly world in which it lives.

Easily maintained by mowing, this labyrinth (TOP) combines brick pavers and fieldstone flush with the earth.

A very large labyrinth can be laid out in a grassy field (BOTTOM LEFT) and change course with the movement of a few stones.

Some believe that labyrinths in shady, tree-protected spaces (BOTTOM RIGHT) contain greater energy within.

Creating a Labyrinth

Gardeners who use a dowsing rod to find water will sometimes also use one to help divine the place with the best convergence of energy for their labyrinth. Yet such an approach is best balanced with practical considerations as well. Shady sites mean less competition from weeds, though you will also be limited in the plants you can grow. As a preemptive strike against weeds in a sunny site, cover the ground with perforated black plastic blanketed with 3 inches of mulch before creating your labyrinth.

You will need a circle at least 40 feet across, though the actual amount of space needed varies with the width of the paths, which can be from 18 to 36 inches wide. When outlining the labyrinth with stone, you must also allow 6 inches or so for the interior lines within your labyrinth. As an example, you would need about 3 tons of medium-sized stones (less than 10 pounds each) to define the lines of a Seven Circuit labyrinth with 18-inch-wide paths. (Other basic designs are the Eleven Circuit and the Twelve Circuit.) Rounded river stones are perfect because of the way they naturally seem to belong on the soil's surface.

Begin by studying the pattern on paper, drawing it several times with a pencil. When you feel that you understand the structure, lay the first four stones, called the seed stones, in a perfect square. Then mark your labyrinth on the ground using cornmeal, flour, or a mixture of the two. For a labyrinth 40 feet across, you may need at least 15 pounds to make a clear outline, but the marking process will take only a few minutes.

Next, walk the labyrinth a few times, at different times of the day, to make sure you are comfortable with its location, its orientation, and the widths of the paths. Then begin laying the stones, which do not need to be firmly set into the soil but can simply be laid on top, as you will be walking on the ground between them. Take your time with this step, placing stones you especially like at turns or broad places in large curves. You may also want to leave a few spaces for plants to make your labyrinth feel more natural and grounded. In addition to using tough little paving plants, it's quite effective to plug in dwarf annuals such as lobelia or sweet alyssum, or stud small spaces with little bulbs such as dwarf daffodil or snowdrops. Place taller plants along the outside of the labyrinth to give it a feeling of enclosure.

Meandering Meditation

There is no right or wrong way to do walking meditation. However, it helps to take a moment to focus by standing at the entrance to the labyrinth and taking a few slow, deep breaths. Some people like to take a question with them, which can be directed to God, to your inner self, or to whatever you think of as spirit. If you don't know what to ask, try this: "Is there anything I need to know right now?" An answer may not come immediately, but you can be assured, it will come. ■

The dry conditions and good drainage in deep crevices create an ideal habitat for herbs such as thyme and creeping oregano.

Fragrance Underfoot

Is it a pathway or a garden? A stone walkway in which numerous crevices give rise to pretty plants always begs the question, especially in summer, when fragrant herbs and flowers are at their peak. But in winter, when most of the plants recede into dormancy, the stones take over the scene, and the notion that the place is, indeed, a garden fades to a whisper.

The concept of a stone walkway that also supports plants is open to endless interpretations, with one or the other element receiving primary emphasis. If the stones are set over soil, with only enough sand or paver base beneath them to help keep them level, you can even change things from year to year, adding and subtracting stones or plants according to your gardening plans for the coming season. Some gardeners find such delight in having plants arise between stones that they find places for them everywhere, including the center of the walkway, so that actually using the corridor forces you to take a series of mincing steps. Yet logic and reason suggest that all upright plants should be limited to the walkway's outer edges, with only ground-hugging dwarfs allowed to claim the middle ground.

One garden theme that has widespread appeal is the potager's garden, a French concept that translates as "soup maker's garden." Such a garden might feature a walkway with tough little flavoring herbs, such as various thymes and creeping oregano, which stay close to the ground near the crevices in which they are planted. More upright culinary herbs, such as basil, chives, parsley, rosemary, and sage, would typically skirt the pathway's edges. Using such a walkway is an adventure in fragrance as leaves that are stepped upon or brushed against release their intoxicating aromas.

For many gardeners, the greatest challenge of creating a walkway that prominently includes plants is to avoid the appearance of messy chaos. One obvious approach is to limit crevice plants to one or two species, such as creeping thyme in sun or sweet woodruff in shade. Then, along the edges, you can organize plants according to a rhythmic, linear plan. Place like plants on opposite sides of the walkway, so they appear to echo each other across the path. Include an intermittent edging of curly parsley, dwarf basil, mound-forming dianthus, or other naturally neat plants. Finally, since paving stone is often gray, broaden the color band by growing drifts of artemisia, dusty miller, sage, or other gray-foliage plants along the walkway's edges.

Keep in mind that during the winter you will be looking at bare stone. Because of this, some type of pattern in the placement of the stone will be welcome, so it's wise to keep your ideas about plants on the back burner until the walkway itself takes shape. To allow for future changes, compose the walkway so that large stones occupy the center, with smaller stones nearer the edges where you are more likely to place plants. It's much easier to lift a small stone to pop in a plant than to custom fit a stone into a hole that insists on sprouting up in weeds.

As much as I would like to tell you that this type of garden is easy to plant and maintain, this is simply not true. Because of the way stones hold on to heat in summer and cold in winter, finding plants that are happy in any particular site is often a trial-and-error process. The plants described on pages 74 to 77 are a good place to start, but you should also visit public gardens in your area to learn about well-adapted species and cultivars. Of course, when you do find a plant that likes your walkway, you are wise to capitalize on this discovery by planting it more widely.

Weeds also can be a nuisance, and I don't consider chemical control to be a reasonable option when edible plants are grown nearby. If you let weeds grow too long, their roots become so extensive that you can easily pull stones loose while weeding, so the only solution is to weed early and often, all the while plugging in plants that grow so tenaciously that they cover places where weeds would otherwise appear.

Winterizing Your Walkway

When you make any type of stone walkway over a shallow bed of sand, or directly in the soil, there is a risk that freezing and thawing during the winter will cause stones to pop out of place. Assume you will have a little repair work to do each spring. This is easily achieved by prying up misplaced stones with a pry bar, adjusting their position by redistributing the rock dust beneath them, and pressing them back into place. If you have many perennial plants growing between the stones that would benefit from winter protection, mulch over both the plants and the walkway with 3 to 4 inches of straw in early winter, after the ground freezes. In spring, the weathered straw will make wonderful mulch elsewhere in your garden. In walkways that are left unmulched, never use salt or other chemicals to melt ice, because accumulated salt can seriously harm the plants growing in the crevices. ■

Corsican Mint *(Mentha requienii)*

Most mints are so aggressive that they will quickly overtake a walkway, but not little Corsican mint, which features dainty, ¼-inch-wide green leaves that grow into a fine-textured mat less than 1 inch tall, topped by light purple flowers in midsummer. Adapted in Zones 6 to 9, this mint requires excellent drainage and tends to suffer in extreme heat with no break from the midday sun. It offers fine minty fragrance, so it's worth trying in different spots to find a place that suits its needs perfectly.

Dwarf Mondo Grass *(Ophiopogon japonicus)*

When grown between crevices in a formal stone walkway, dwarf mondo grass, with its dark green, grasslike foliage, leaves little to be desired. Evergreen, uniform, and nearly maintenance free, this plant's only limitation is winter hardiness, which varies from Zone 5 to 7, depending on cultivar. All are willing to stand heat to Zone 10. Look for neat, compact, 3-inch-tall 'Nana' and silver mist mondo grass *(O. japonicus* 'Variegatus') (shown here).

Creeping Oregano *(Origanum vulgare* 'Compactum')

This spicy herb needs full sun and good drainage, but few crevice plants have as much to offer in terms of fragrance and longevity. Adapted in Zones 3 to 10, the plants become dormant in winter except in mild climates, where they are often evergreen, darkening to a purplish color in cold weather. The dainty flowers produced in midsummer attract bees and other beneficial insects. Also known as dwarf oregano, the variety shown here is 'Compactum'.

Pearlwort *(Sagina subulata)*

Often called Irish moss, pearlwort has fine-textured, 1-inch-tall foliage that does indeed resemble moss, though it is not. This versatile gound cover looks fantastic with sandstone, limestone, or even granite. Pearlwort bears tiny white flowers in midsummer. Adapted in Zones 5 to 8, it needs full sun in the North and partial shade in the South. It also benefits from regular moisture and a gritty soil. Humid heat gives pearlwort trouble, as does extreme drought.

Soapwort (*Saponaria* 'Bressingham')

Originally from the meadows and rocky, mountainous areas of Europe and southwest Asia, soapwort requires gritty, sharply drained soil. The hybrid 'Bressingham' grows to 3 inches high, and its many short-stemmed cymes carry brilliant deep-pink flowers. It is adapted for Zones 5 to 8. Besides poking out of a walkway, soapwort is also a good choice for growing in rock gardens and in stone troughs. Its common name refers to the fact that its leaves can be used to create a mild soap.

Sedum (*Sedum spurium*)

Tiny sedums suitable for growing in crevices are numerous, so don't feel that you need to be limited by species names. Any cultivar that hugs the ground and grows no higher than 4 inches when it's in full flower is worth trying. One of the sedums known as two-row stone crops, 'Red Carpet' (shown here), with its deep red stems, leaves, and flowers, blooms throughout the summer and is only 3 to 4 inches tall. Set out plants in spring, and expect them to spread slowly for the first couple of years. This species thrives in Zones 4 to 9.

Woolly Thyme (*Thymus pseudolaniginosus*)

Expect confusion in botanical names when shopping for woolly thyme, which goes under several names. All varieties have soft gray-green foliage that grows to less than 4 inches high, spreading into mats in hospitable places that have excellent drainage and some protection from baking sun. Adapted in Zones 4 to 9, this thyme releases a refreshing herbal scent when crushed underfoot. After the small blooms wither in midsummer, shear the plants back to help them maintain a tight cover of foliage.

CHAPTER 3

MAKING ASSETS OF HILLS AND DIPS

Hills and dips captivate us with their subtle intrigue, and changes in elevation naturally divide different parts of the garden. In this chapter, we will look at two ways to employ stone in sites that are not on the

level — building stone steps into serious inclines and using stone to stabilize places where the force of water creates chronic problems. Very hilly sites badly need these kinds of stone features, but every garden can make use of the drama that comes from a short run of low steps or a dry streambed lined with stone.

Broad slab steps provide a leisurely transition between levels and also double as viewing platforms within a garden painted in shades of lavender and purple.

Ascent and Descent: Design Objectives

When designing with stone on multiple levels, take some time to consider the differences between going up and going down, because how you experience any part of a landscape is strongly affected by ascent and descent. When climbing, we tend to move slowly, noticing every small detail, savoring the journey out of necessity. This is true whether we are going up two steps or ten, and we always tend to linger at the top, perhaps to give ourselves a little reward.

When going down, we move much faster, often bypassing interesting or beautiful things that are right before our eyes. Indeed, we tend to look down on our feet, so we are more likely to notice the colors and textures of the stones that are helping us along our way. The implication here is that we are more likely to enjoy plantings and features viewed from eye level when we are climbing, and we are drawn toward details of textures and patterns situated on or near the ground as we descend.

We also have unconscious expectations of what awaits us after we arrive at a new level. When we've climbed, we are naturally delighted by surroundings that feel light and airy, conjuring up the aura of a mountaintop complete with a panoramic view. There we like to find a comfortable platform of some type, which might be a small lawn or sitting area that feels removed from the rest of the landscape. At the end of a downward trek, we like a sense of cozy enclosure. One way to provide this is to accent the heavy feel of a low spot with thick, lush plantings of shrubs and foliage plants. This is simply mimicking what you might find in wild, natural spaces—airy sparseness at high elevations and jungle-thick closeness in low spots.

Sizing Up Steps

In the interest of continuity, the width of steps should generally match that of any walkway or landing to which they are linked. However, rather than follow this guideline absolutely, you may wish to manipulate the proportions of your steps to enhance the uniqueness of your landscape and the way you want to use steps to connect different areas within it. For example, steps that narrow slightly just before they arrive at a raised platform garden increase the anticipation, echoing the sensation you might have when climbing a mountain until the path opens to a vista. When steps descend to a low spot, a broadening feels more inviting, because we naturally expect a wide, flat valley at the bottom of an incline.

The purpose of a very short run of only two or three steps may be very different. In this situation, the steps are intended to be as aesthetic as they are practical, because their main job is to announce a change. The louder the announcement, the more impact it has, and the best way to maximize impact is to make the steps as broad as possible. You also can increase the resonance of a short run of steps by using stone with surprising color or texture, or by adding a gate, arbor, or pillar to transform the steps into a special entryway that cannot possibly escape notice.

If part of your landscape slopes upward or downward very slightly, with a measured rise of only 10 to 15 inches, you can create a natural division using stone steps with an adjoining stone retaining wall. The creation of this fixed tier will level the two areas, making them suitable for either garden or lawn.

Craggy stone steps cut a pathway up a fern-covered hillside (FAR LEFT). Low risers make them easy to negotiate.

Even a small rise between garden areas is enhanced by several shallow steps and a low retaining wall (RIGHT).

Studying the Site

Before deciding on a plan to make a slope more accessible with stone steps, study the site and imagine different ways that steps might accomplish the task at hand. Your steps need not cut straight up a slope. In fact, the more serious the incline, the wiser it may be to angle steps across the slope or even lay them out in a zigzag pattern. Steep slopes that include a number of steps are best broken up by landings — broad resting spots along the climb that are roomy enough so that a person can pause and turn around comfortably. Always break up runs of more than six steps with a landing. If your steps go up a slope diagonally or change direction along the way, turns are always logical places to locate landings.

If you plan to combine steps with stone walls or stone-lined beds, it's important to get the steps situated first. If the site is very rocky, you may find that you need to adjust the layout of your steps as you work around big buried boulders, which will in turn affect adjoining walls or beds you add later.

Once you know where your steps will go, you can measure the site to figure out how many steps you will need. Doing math is part of this process, but don't be intimidated by the fact that you will need to work out certain numbers on paper. It's quite straightforward, and it's the only way you'll be able to estimate your need for materials, time, and possibly outside help as well.

You will need two sets of numbers to arrive at reliable step-building estimates: measurements of your slope and measurements of the size of the individual steps that you plan to build.

The steps at this site were laid up before the oversize stones of the retaining wall were put in place. Broader treads at each sixth step provide a place to pause.

Step Math

The two numbers that you need when planning to build steps are the rise and the run of the slope. The rise is the change in vertical elevation from the bottom of the slope to the top, while the run is the horizontal distance between the beginning of your steps and where you want them to end. If you have a helper to hold one end of a long measuring tape, you can easily get both numbers.

Have your helper hold the end of the tape at ground level at the top of the slope while you stand at the bottom (or at the place where you know you will be locating a landing). Use a carpenter's level and a 2x4 (if you have one long enough) to hold the tape perfectly horizontal, and measure its distance (see drawing A). This is the run. Continue to hold your end of the tape at the height where it's level with the top of the slope (it helps to hold it against your body). Then have your helper scramble down and measure from your end of the tape to the ground at the bottom of the slope; this is the rise.

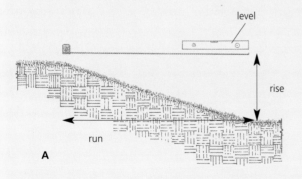

A

Next, you need to work out tread and riser measurements for your steps. The tread is the flat part of the step where you place your foot, with a minimum acceptable depth of 12 inches (from toe to heel). For a garden, you may want a much deeper tread, up to 24 inches. The riser is the vertical lift between steps, and it can range from 5 to 8 inches, though 5 to 6 inches is usually the

most comfortable for outdoors (see drawing B). You can vary the depth of the tread somewhat from step to step. Not so with the riser, which should be exactly the same for each step. This is what our minds and feet come to expect, so varying the riser by an inch or two, so that one step is 4 inches high and the next one is 5 or 6, is an invitation to stumble.

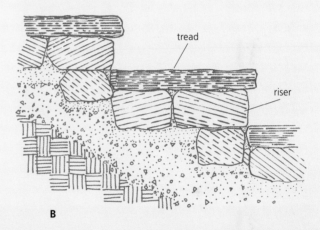

B

To determine precisely how many steps you will need to comfortably facilitate the climb, divide the total rise of the slope by the riser height you prefer. To determine the depth of each tread, divide the run by the number of steps you have just calculated. If necessary, modify your plan by changing the layout of your steps or by adjusting the precise riser height and tread depth, until you are satisfied that the steps you are building will be functional, attractive, and fun to use.

For example, if you want to build steps up a slope with a 6-foot (72-inch) run and a 3-foot (36-inch) rise, first divide the rise by 6 inches, the ideal lift outdoors. This indicates that you need six steps. Next, divide the total run, 72 inches, by the number of steps, 6, to find that the treads should be 12 inches deep.

Choosing Materials for Steps

Because steps have to be stable, not wobbly, they should ideally be made of thick, large stones. In other words, heavy stones. For this reason, building dry-laid stone steps is not a good project if you have a delicate back, or if you have nobody to help when hundred-pound slabs must be pushed into place. There are several ways around this problem, the most common of which is to carefully stack medium-sized flat stones into steps, with the largest stones you can handle placed on top as the actual tread surfaces. If you are buying several tons of stacking stone to use for multiple projects, you may be able to pick through the pile and collect enough large, flat stones for this use. However,

many stoneyards set aside very large flat stones, called slabs, which may be well worth their cost and difficulty of handling because they make such wonderful steps.

Other alternatives to handling massive stones include framing steps with wood or other materials and then topping them with stone. A favorite approach among contractors is to build the steps of concrete block and then top them with flagstone. However, because the stones used this way are not extremely heavy, they must be mortared into place. And they rarely have the authentic, organic look needed to complement other stone structures, such as stacked walls or raised beds.

An overhanging slab steals the show in an intricately built wall-step combination that doubles as a poolside patio.

Softening the Edges

Before you actually start building stone steps, decide on what you will do to dress the finished edges of the steps. Whenever you can, it's good to set stones on their edges along the outside of the steps. This holds back soil that would otherwise wash down and make steps muddy. These edging stones need not be flat; in fact, rounded stones will work well and look lovely, provided they are firmly planted. Where this approach is not practical or you prefer using plants, get plants situated as promptly as possible, before heavy rains turn the sides of your steps into ugly gullies.

Because steps always include straight edges, it is often soothing to soften them up a bit with plants that have fine-textured foliage, or at least a gently sprawling growth habit. A variety of choice plants for this job are described on pages 96 to 99. And if the edges of your steps are sufficiently stabilized with stone, you always have the option of accessorizing them with plants grown in containers. Add seasonal color with pots of moss verbena, cascading white petunias, or other flowers you love. This is a good reason to build wide steps, so that you won't crowd the interior of the steps with pots and other things that you can easily trip over.

Step Lighting

Many people find steps tricky enough to negotiate in the daytime, and steps can be downright treacherous when cloaked in darkness. Provide some kind of lighting for your steps, especially turns or landings that might be easy to miss. If outdoor lighting from your house cannot be adjusted to fill this need, you can install low-wattage electric circuit lights along your steps, or spend a little more for solar-powered pedestal lights specially designed for walkways and other outdoor areas.

In the Chinese style (TOP), stone steps are nearly hidden, giving a sense of mystery ahead. A short run of single-slab steps (MIDDLE) makes for firm footing. Cut stone steps (BOTTOM) are flanked by offset plantings of flowers.

Setting Stone Steps

You must always build steps from the bottom up, with the front lip of each step resting firmly on the step below it. Violate this rule, and you will never have solid steps.

Stone steps need the same foundation you would use for a stone walkway: about 4 to 6 inches of processed gravel, topped by 2 inches of paver base on which to lay the steps. Begin by removing any large roots or other obstructions from the step-building site. Unless you suspect that large boulders lurk beneath the surface, wait to excavate the area for each step until you have set the step immediately beneath. Plan ahead for a place to put excavated soil, which is best carted away in a wheelbarrow to a nearby spot.

Lay the Bottom Tier

Beginning at the bottom of the slope, dig out vegetation and soil to an 8- to 12-inch depth, then fill with the processed gravel and rock dust layers to make a platform for your base step. With this and all other steps, it is best to have the foundation pitch forward very slightly, so that the back of the step is about ¼ inch higher than the front edge. Steps with a very slight forward pitch shed water, leaves, and other debris more easily than steps that are absolutely level.

Set the stones for the bottom tier flush with surrounding surfaces so you can mow over them. Keep crevices as tight as possible to give the illusion that the base is composed of a single large expanse of stone.

Lay the First Step

Now excavate the place for the first step, including the area for the gravel and rock dust foundation layers.

Set the riser stones in place, using large, heavy stones for the bottom tier, and positioning them so that their front edges join evenly and tightly and rest firmly on the back of the base step.

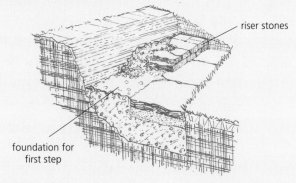

riser stones

foundation for first step

Go Easy on Yourself

Building stone steps isn't nearly as difficult as you might think, especially if you take advantage of a few basic tips:

▶ Even though you work from the bottom up, stockpile stones and other materials at the top of the slope, because it's much easier to move heavy things downhill than it is to drag them up an incline.

▶ A couple of stout boards come in handy to use as a ramp to move large stones from the top of the slope to where they are needed.

▶ As you work your way up, you can save a lot of cleanup time by laying a tarp over the lower steps after they are set in place. Otherwise, you can't help but scatter lots of dirt over the finished steps as you dig out the places for those higher on the slope. ▪

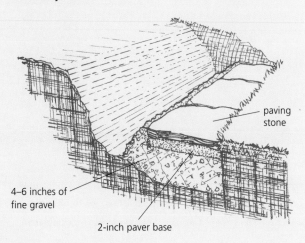

paving stone

4–6 inches of fine gravel

2-inch paver base

Top the riser stones with large flat stones for the actual treads. Set tread stones so that any joints are offset from joints in the riser stones. If needed, trim the fronts of the tread stones to remove small protrusions. As you complete each step, jump around on it a bit to make sure it is absolutely stable. The addition of the next step will help further press it into place but will not make up for major wobbles or gaps.

Use a carpenter's level to make sure the step is level from side to side and has a very slight forward pitch. Finally, stand back and take a good look at your work. If the step is not quite right, remove the stones and start over, using small shims if needed to make the stones sit and fit exactly right (see "Setting Shims" at right).

When you're satisfied with the step, fill all crevices with paver base or a mixture of paver base and soil, jamming it into place with a metal rod. If you are planning to build a wall adjoining the steps, don't fill in along the sides of the steps until later, when wall construction gets under way. Note that although the tread stones must cover the entire area, it's okay to fill small spaces behind the riser

stones with smaller stones surrounded by firmly packed gravel or paver base. This is a good use for cobbles gathered from your pile that are just the right size to serve as reinforcements at the back of the steps.

Cover the step you've just built with a tarp or scrap lumber to keep it clean, and excavate the site for the next step.

Complete Additional Steps

Use the same procedure, and pay close attention to the combined heights of your riser stones and tread stones, so that the second step has exactly the same rise as the first. Although it's wonderful if the riser stones fit tightly together, this is not absolutely necessary, since they will be covered by the broad, flat tread stones. However, it is crucial that each riser stone rests on the back of the step below it and forms a solid foundation for the tread stones. Again, you may find that you need shims to get a good, solid fit.

Repeat this procedure for all the steps. If you are planning a retaining wall but can't begin it right away, do take a few minutes to loosely set stones along the sides of your steps to keep the soil from shifting about until it is stabilized by stone.

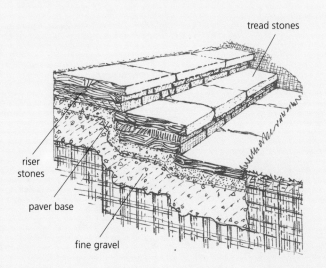

tread stones

riser stones

paver base

fine gravel

Mixing It Up

Rot-resistant logs or railroad ties look very much at home among stone steps in informal areas. You can use them to frame steps that utilize flat stone for the interior tread surfaces, or break up a series of many stone steps with deeper landings structured with wood. Wood-framed steps also can be great problem solvers when you don't have just the right stone for a certain spot or must bypass slab stones because they're simply too bulky for you to handle. And when you're trying to tame a particularly steep slope, it is easier to "cut into" the hillside with long logs or railroad ties than with huge slabs of stone.

From an aesthetic point of view, wood risers naturally echo the colors and textures of dark tree trunks and surface roots, making them look very natural when incorporated into a series of rustic stone steps. Wood combines with stone beautifully in woodland areas, where you might expect to see woody tree roots wandering about among stones — this is the illusion created when wood and stone are teamed together in the construction of steps.

Partnering Wood and Stone

Logs, railroad ties, or landscape timbers are of sufficient size to form the full risers of steps, but they are not deep enough to create a roomy tread. You can use an endless variety of stone to fill the narrow space behind each wood riser, which may be a strip only a few inches deep. Small rectangular stones may be laid in a symmetrical pattern, or you can arrange rounded cobbles for a natural look that appears to have come straight out of the woods. This is a good use for small, thick stones that point down into the soil when laid on edge, though you may need a small pick to dig out places for them. Small stones that are deeply set won't pop out of place as the soil freezes and thaws, which is always a risk when you pave any space with small flat stones.

Begin by excavating the horizontal surface for the lowest wood riser, allowing enough foundation space to spread about an inch of gravel under the log or railroad tie. Also excavate soil behind the riser space, removing only about 3 inches of soil — just enough

Leveling a Log

Large logs can easily be sculpted into risers for steps if you don't mind doing a little work with a saw and wood chisel. Choose logs of a uniform size that are of a hard, durable species, such as cedar, locust, hickory or oak, and have them cut to the width of your steps plus at least 3 inches on each end (many skilled woodcutters will be glad to have this job). Sculpt a flat side into the center of each log by using a saw or chain saw to cut a series of notches into the least knotty side of the log, 2 inches apart and 2 inches deep. Then use a hammer and wood chisel to chunk out the notches and smooth the surface below and between them. ■

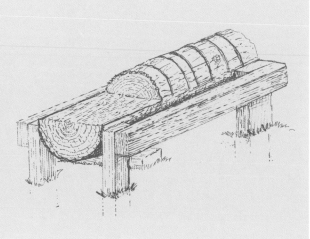

Landscape timbers can be used to make sturdy low risers for broad, gravel-filled treads.

so that you can fill it in with a bed of fine gravel or paver base topped by whatever stone you plan to use. When you're finished digging out the place for the first step, make a horizontal notch where the riser will go, with a flat area behind it that reaches from midway up the riser to the back of the step.

Set the wood riser in place, arranging gravel beneath it as needed to make it lie firmly in place and fit snugly against the lip of soil behind it. Use a carpenter's level to make sure it is level from side to side and has a very slight pitch from back to front. Reinforce the riser with rebar stakes (see box at right), and then spread 2 inches of paver base for your stonework behind it. Install stones, firmly pack crevices, and then move up to the next step.

When all of your steps are built, dress the edges with plants. If the ends of the risers are buried, the pockets behind the ends are ideal for trailing plants such as mazus or periwinkle. Or you can use stone to frame planting boxes at the ends of wood risers, fill them with soil, and plug in mound-forming plants such as lamium (in shade) or creeping phlox or thyme, if the site is drenched in sun.

Reinforced Risers

When using any type of wooden step risers, you have the luxury of securing them in place with metal reinforcing bars called rebar stakes. Simply drill holes into the ends of the logs or timbers using a power drill with an extension bit, and pound in the rebar after the risers are set in place but before any stones are installed on top of or behind the risers. ■

Solving Drainage Problems

Because water always flows downhill, the area at the base of steps often becomes a natural basin for moisture. By its nature, an expanse of unmortared stone helps accumulated water dissipate, because water can easily filter through the crevices between the stones to the subsoil below. However, low areas that receive large loads of water may benefit from special features that make drainage more efficient. Depending on the volume of water an area can be expected to receive and the style of your landscape, you can choose among Japanese surface drains, underground French drains, or special grading that directs excess water toward a stone-lined swale or a dry streambed.

One simple concept to keep in mind is that the more crevices that exist between stones, the more opportunities there are for water to seep through to the deepest layers of soil. Places paved with large pieces of flagstone tend to create what is called sheet runoff, in which excess water flows over the surface and down toward the lowest edge. Once the soil becomes fully saturated, sheet runoff will occur from surfaces paved with smaller stones, too, often taking with it loose gravel, paver base, or sand used to fill the crevices.

French Drains

A French drain is a buried section of drainage pipe, surrounded by gravel, that collects excess water and carries it away from areas such as basements and walkways. The more your landscape slopes, the more likely you are to discover the need for one or more French drains as you are planning and building your garden. The base of steps, the edges of a low patio, and any disturbed area that is higher than your house are logical places to install a French drain. The goal is always to make sure that any water that might flow toward your house is intercepted and diverted to an area where it can do no harm.

Although some people hide a French drain from view completely by planting shallow-rooted grass over it, you can top the drain with loose stone as well. This approach is particularly pleasing if the drain connects to a stone-lined water run or dry creek bed. Whether the drain is visible or not, the ends of the pipe do need to follow a downward route to a low area. And, in the interest of community cooperation, they should not empty into a neighbor's property; this is inconsiderate and often illegal. Another possibility for solving this problem—creating rivers of stone such as swales or dry streambeds — is discussed on pages 92 to 95.

Perforated Drainage Pipe

Inexpensive and easy to handle, black perforated drainage pipe comes in 4- and 6-inch diameters. Short sections of this accordion-like pipe can be locked together, or you can buy long pieces in rolls. Slits along the sides and bottom of the pipe collect water, so that the pipe works like a little underground river. To keep soil from collecting in the slits, loosely wrap the pipe in landscape fabric before installing it in any type of subsurface drain. If you need only a short length of drainage pipe, one alternative is to cut a piece of 3-inch-diameter PVC pipe to the right length and riddle the bottom and sides of the pipe with holes made with a power drill or a series of parallel cuts made with a saw. ■

Japanese Surface Drains

Increasing the number of crevices between stones in order to allow greater surface area for drainage is the basic idea behind Japanese surface drains. This type of drain usually includes a buried section of perforated drainage pipe, much as a French drain does. In some cases, the Japanese drain may instead use a pebble-filled reservoir similar to a dry well to allow water to disperse. The part we see above ground is a seam of closely spaced small stones located in the lowest part of the paved surface. What appears to be a pretty pattern in stone is actually the top of a drain in which small stones are set on edge perpendicular to the flow of water. Placing stones this way slows the flow, increasing the amount of water that percolates down into the drain.

A Japanese drain is a great approach to use when creating a stone patio or landing that has only a minimal grade away from the house or that flattens out sooner than it should. The procedure for building a Japanese drain is quite straightforward. As you excavate the site, dig a drainage trench down its lowest part, gradually making it deeper as it moves away from the area to be paved, toward a lower site. The trench may be only 8 inches deep at its deepest point, and it should drop at least ¼ inch per foot as it moves away from the house, patio, or landing. Line the bottom of the trench with 2 inches of gravel, and then set in a length of perforated drainage pipe. Cover the pipe with a layer of gravel up to 2 inches below surface level. Install the stonework around the sides of the drainage area first, and then pave over the drainage seam at the middle with small stones laid on edge, as shown in the drawing at right.

What could be simply a drainage ditch here becomes a lively landscape feature, artfully patterned and edged with stone.

Functional, Decorative Drainage

A Japanese drain can promote drainage on a level site, while at the same time adding a striking design element to a flagstone patio.

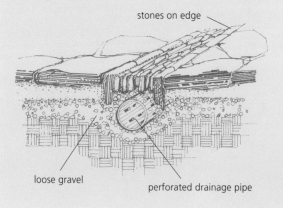

stones on edge

loose gravel

perforated drainage pipe

Rivers of Stone

Once upon a time, low places in landscapes, where rainwater accumulates until it flows away, were simply called ditches, and nobody liked them. Reputed to host snakes and mosquitoes, ditches were simply endured because there seemed to be no other option, but that's no longer true. With the addition of the right kind of stone, ditches and swales have been promoted to the status of landscape features. In fact, ribbons of stone that meander through a landscape do such an effective job of conjuring up a streambed that gardeners often look for opportunities to include them in their landscape plans.

Whether or not water is actually present, a curving river of stone suggests water and its inexorable movement. A rock-lined swale or dry streambed can be purely aesthetic or completely practical. For instance, a dry streambed might gently wind through your landscape, perhaps stopping at a water feature along the way, so that it looks like it existed long before any other part of your garden, or even

your house. It will work this magic especially well if you arrange for it to curve gently through the landscape, rounding large trees naturally, with clumps of plants adorning its edges so that they appear to be held back by the rush of invisible water. Or, situated in a low spot, a streambed may mimic a broad wash or marsh, where small rounded stones and pebbles are naturally inclined to accumulate.

On the practical side, a sunken river of stone can help channel excess water away from your house or garden. In addition to carrying the water that naturally flows through the site, a rock-lined swale or streambed can receive water from French drains, including water that runs off the roof of your house. You can even use it to direct water toward your garden if you live in a climate where rain is scarce. However you use it, a stylish stone swale will enrich your landscape with imaginary movement, even when it is as dry as a bone.

Observe your property closely during a heavy rain, and you will get plenty of ideas of where and how you can put a man-made streambed to good use. Where does water tend to carve gullies? Where is the flow fastest? Are there places that drain more slowly, so that they sit in mud long after the rain has ended? If you create a dry streambed, are there places where pathways will cross it? What kinds of plants can you use to evoke exactly the kind of scene you want?

Lined with flat stones, a shallow drainage ditch (LEFT) imitates a meandering stream in a woodland garden. Runoff at the bottom of this hillside (RIGHT) once created a muddy area after heavy rains until a stone channel was built to direct water away. Even in dry periods, the streambed makes a pleasing frame for the rock garden above.

Stone for Swales

To maintain the illusion that nothing wants to grow in the swale because of the presence of rushing water, excavate the site as needed so you can line it with at least 4 inches of stone. A shallow cover of stone will allow weeds to flourish, which can be a problem in areas that receive plenty of sun. Many weeds will be seriously set back if you line the swale with landscape fabric before filling it with stone.

When water runs over stones in nature, it makes them rounded in shape. This is a very slow process that takes hundreds of years, and meanwhile other pieces of stone enter the river or stream, broken from nearby outcroppings or pushed up from below, retaining their large size and angular edges. So a natural river run invariably includes small rounded stones and larger craggy ones. Not surprisingly, the most attractive simulated streambeds use exactly these mixtures of materials.

How you balance these two types of stone depends on the site and the mood you wish to create. Sudden changes in elevation, such as drop-offs, are logical places to put large stones that won't be easily moved by rushing water. Wide, comparatively level spots can be filled with smaller rounded stones; for interest, mix in a few larger ones taken from streams where they have already been shaped by water. If you value formal symmetry in the part of your landscape where a streambed is needed, limit yourself to one or two types of stone, with the largest stones placed along the edges and the smaller ones in the center. Sharply defined changes in texture, such as rounded stones arranged in a ribbon alongside broken pieces of shale, will also give a dry streambed a more managed appearance.

Whenever possible, make sure that the stone in your streambed repeats a stone type used in other parts of your landscape. The streambed is such an elemental feature, seeming to have been carved out of the ground naturally, that despite its quiet demeanor, it should always merge and flow with other stone features and with the plants that surround it.

Because fast-moving water has no trouble moving small stones, it's important to either edge a swale with medium to large stones or include big stones prominently in the mix. This is less of a concern in sites that will seldom be flooded or that are flanked by thick vegetation.

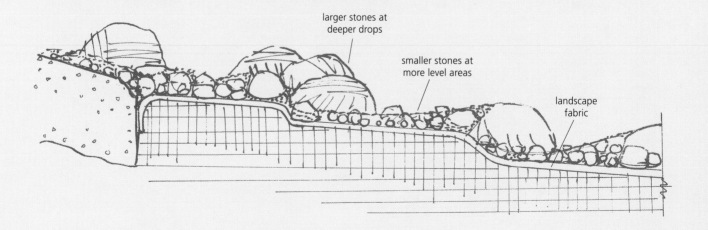

larger stones at deeper drops

smaller stones at more level areas

landscape fabric

Deepening the Theme

Because a dry streambed evokes the feeling of water, whether or not it is actually present, plants that might grow naturally at the water's edge add impact, while marrying the stone-lined water run to its site. Use upright reeds and grasses for vertical interest, interspersed with low-growing ground covers that seem to creep toward an imagined source of moisture. In dry sites, drifts of light-textured plants such as sea lavender can appear to float among the stones. A shady site will seem most natural lined with coarse rhododendrons underplanted with ferns.

The objective is to make a dry streambed (or a wet one, for that matter) appear to be natural. Use plants to exaggerate the feeling of flow, just as the stones magnify the suggestion of running water.

Stepping-Stones and Bridges

A pathway that crosses a dry streambed presents an unusual opportunity to conjure up a crossing through the use of stepping-stones, a flat stone slab held slightly aloft with sturdy rocks, or even a large log with its top side carved flat for easy walking. You do not have to need a crossing to create one. An arching bridge over a dry streambed is just plain fun to use, and walking across a series of flat stepping-stones set in a sea of stone feels almost like dancing.

Large drifts of iris and daylilies combine with juniper to form a naturally graceful edge along the streambed.

Plants for Steps and Swales

Slopes and low areas are excellent places to use rangy plants that like to wander about until they find sheltered spots, where they dig in and prosper, filling holes and crevices with attractive foliage. Plants grown on steps are naturally restrained by foot traffic, and those grown in swales may be subject to repeated flooding, so they seldom get out of hand when accompanied by these pressures. And, although some of the plants included here do produce colorful blooms once a year, they enrich the garden with their foliage and texture over a long season, and sometimes year-round.

When setting plants in locations that are prone to erosion, you may need to baby them at first to help them become established. Dig secure planting pockets amended with rich compost, and arrange stones around new plantings to hold the soil in place until new roots have a chance to develop.

Even when these plants have been in the ground for years, shallow roots are the rule rather than the exception. To keep from accidentally pulling them up, always use sharp pruning shears when trimming them back or cleaning up old growth that has been damaged by cold.

Ajuga (*Ajuga reptans*)

Often called bugleweed or carpet bugleweed, ajuga is evergreen where winters are mild and becomes dormant in winter in colder climates. Adapted in Zones 3 to 9, in either sun or partial shade, ajuga forms round rosettes that multiply as the mother plants send out stems that root and grow into new rosettes. Flower spikes appear in spring. 'Catlin's Giant' (shown here) has 6-inch-long, purplish leaves and spikey flowers that grow to 8 inches tall.

Bunchberry (*Cornus canadensis*)

The tiniest member of the dogwood family, bunchberry grows only 6 inches tall, and it spreads slowly via underground rhizomes. White spring flowers give way to bright red berries in fall; glossy green leaves in summer turn red in the fall. Bunchberry is ideal for shady spots in the cool climates of Zones 2 to 7. It requires rich, acid soil, so prepare planting spots by digging in plenty of peat moss or leaf mold. Mulch between plants with pine needles to keep the soil cool and moist.

Myrtle Spurge *(Euphorbia myrsinites)*

The same ironclad constitution that makes this little spurge at home among stone steps has earned it a place on some state lists of noxious weeds, so don't let it get out of hand. Keeping it under control is easily accomplished simply by snipping off the chartreuse-yellow flower clusters in early summer, before they develop seeds. Drought tolerant and willing to grow in either sun or partial shade, myrtle spurge features sprawling stems clad with blue-gray foliage. It is easily grown in Zones 5 to 8.

Wintergreen *(Gaultheria procumbens)*

A tiny treasure native to northern woods, wintergreen (also called checkerberry) has bright red fruits and glossy, evergreen leaves with a minty scent and flavor. Individual stems grow only 4 to 6 inches high, with no side branches, but they spread to form a loose mat. A shady site with acid soil is needed to grow wintergreen. It's ideal for tucking among large stones or along low steps in Zones 3 to 8. Native plant nurseries are often the best source for starter plants.

English Ivy *(Hedera helix)*

Common, yet infinitely useful, English ivy has a bad reputation because of its tendency to run up buildings and swallow them. It is much better behaved when used as a ground cover over rock-encrusted slopes and steps. Some cultivars are hardy to Zone 4, though English ivy is most at home in Zones 5 to 8. It can be slow to establish unless well-rooted plants are set out in planting pockets that have been well enriched with organic matter. Shown here is 'Silverdust'.

Lamium *(Lamium maculatum)*

Often called by its unflattering common name of spotted deadnettle, *Lamium maculatum* is an outstanding plant for edging stone steps in partial shade. Many cultivars, such as *L. maculatum* f. *album* 'Pale Peril' (shown here), have leaves with silvery white centers, making this plant an outstanding choice for brightening up dark corners. Easily cultivated in Zones 4 to 8, this lamium grows into a mound that slowly spreads outward. Most lamiums bear white or pale pink blossoms in late spring. Shearing the plants back after the flowers fade keeps them handsome through late summer.

Mazus *(Mazus reptans)*

If you have some semishady steps in Zones 5 to 8, this is the first plant to try to nestle into the site. Perfectly suited for use as a small-scale ground cover, mazus will happily leap and bound until it finds exactly the places it likes. Exotic purple blossoms marked with white appear in late spring. Mazus needs steady moisture, but when pleased, it thrives with little care beyond occasional trimming and a light feeding each spring.

Pachysandra *(Pachysandra terminalis)*

Sometimes called Japanese spurge, pachysandra is most at home in shade, in soil rich enough to please flowers. It makes a fine plant to tuck into pockets along the edges of stone steps. Variegated forms are useful near the base of steps, where shade and moisture tend to be abundant. Pachysandra is usually regarded as evergreen in Zones 4 to 8, but unless plants are snow-covered, winter damages them so seriously that they are best cut back in early spring to a height of 2 to 3 inches.

Creeping Phlox *(Phlox subulata)*

Often called moss pink, this is the phlox that covers slopes in pastel blankets of blossoms in midspring, in varying shades of pink, lavender, and white. Willing to grow in wide crevices or soil-filled pockets between stones, creeping phlox requires at least a half day of sun. Hardy to Zone 3, creeping phlox asks for little in terms of soil, though it will struggle in *very* lean sand. Plants set out in early fall can be counted upon to bloom well the following spring.

Creeping Thyme *(Thymus polytrichus* ssp. *britannicus* 'Albus')

Also known as mother-of-thyme, this creeping thyme has somewhat hairy stems and white flowers. Like other thymes, creeping thyme demands predominant sun and excellent drainage, but once established, it should persist for years. Plant it alongside steps or in broad containers stationed near step edges. It is also very effective grown in intermittent drifts along dry streambeds in a sunny spot. It's hardy to Zone 5 and adapted into arid regions of Zone 9.

Creeping Veronica (*Veronica prostrata*)

Herbaceous perennials that are easily grown in Zones 5 to 8, creeping veronicas are low, spreading plants that grow only a few inches tall yet often carpet the ground in an 18-inch-wide mass. In early summer, the plants produce loads of blue or pink blooms, though flower form varies with species. Lavender-pink 'Mrs. Holt' (shown here) is a good choice, but you can also consider other species, such as *V. peduncularis* 'Georgia Blue' and *V. repens* 'Sunshine', which has unusual chartreuse leaves.

Creeping Myrtle (*Vinca minor*)

Also called periwinkle or trailing myrtle, this glossy little evergreen thrives in shade and willingly winds itself around any stones or plants in its path. A real ground hugger, it always stays low and becomes beautifully dressed out each spring with starry blue flowers. Variegated forms are available, along with a few cultivars that bloom white rather than blue. Easily grown in Zones 4 to 9, myrtle also makes a fine trailing plant to slip inside containers planted with annual flowers.

Ferns (numerous species)

Once established, ferns make extremely reliable and long-lived garden plants. Only a few species are evergreen, and, in fact, deciduous ferns that die back in winter often do the best job of producing the lush look that most gardeners want. Check with local nurseries in early spring for ferns known to grow well in your climate. Japanese painted fern (*Athyrium nipponicum* 'Pictum') (shown here) features purple-red stalks and silver-green leaves. It grows in Zones 5 to 8.

CHAPTER 4

THE ROMANCE OF STONE WALLS

Until about 300 years ago, nearly every proper garden was enclosed by a wall, most often one of stone. These walls were intended to exclude roaming animals, but people quickly discovered  that walled gardens were also unmatched as special spaces that felt like little patches of paradise. Today, stone walls are used to mark boundaries and to create beds or niches for beautiful plants, all the while forming ribbons of timeless texture in the landscape.

Long or short, high or low, stone walls define space, serve as handsome architectural elements, and even provide customized beds for plants that might be impossible to grow if not for the existence of the wall.

Dry-stacked walls create numerous planting pockets, ideal if you want a wall that doubles as a vertical garden.

Envisioning Walls

More durable than any other type of fence, stone walls always bring a feeling of permanence to the garden. Whether they are tall enough to support an espalier tree or simply low enclosures for garden beds, stone walls clearly define garden space and securely frame plants grown in their company. You can use stone walls to make a level site more interesting or situate them so that they make slopes more stable and dramatic. Low walls less than 3 feet tall do a good job of establishing boundaries, yet you can see over them to the view beyond.

When planning walls for your landscape, begin with areas where they are most needed. Reasonably small walls, such as those you might build to terrace a slight slope or to frame a bed beneath a specimen tree, are fast and simple to build, so they are great projects for beginners. In places near patios or other activity areas, consider creating a wall that doubles as a bench, increasing your seating space. Walls often are needed to complete a scene in which stone steps or a water garden are featured, especially if the walls flow away from the focal point in a gentle, natural way.

Steer clear of plans that might require walls more than 4 feet high, as these are difficult to build and prone to problems when they are assigned the job of holding back a slope. A series of low terraces usually works better, and it affords more opportunities for gardening as well.

Stone Wall Niches

A plain stone wall is a nice addition to a garden, but one that is colonized by plants is breathtaking to behold. As a place for plants, a wall is also fascinating to work with because of the diversity of secret planting places waiting to be discovered atop, within, and at the base of it.

Stone walls have a way of exaggerating the ecological factors present in a site in ways that we should be able to predict but that sometimes surprise us. For example, the area behind the top of a retaining wall offers superior drainage, but because the wall itself helps retain soil moisture, the site is not particularly dry. Plants that make themselves at home in crevices benefit from protection from wind, yet they also must be able to withstand prolonged chilling when stones freeze solid in winter and extended baking in warm, sunny weather. My favorite niche is the base of

Good wall plants such as moss pink phlox are anchored with deep, moisture-seeking roots, and have small leaves to help withstand dry heat when the sun bakes the stones.

the wall, where moisture, shade, and shelter often give rise to mossy miniature jungles that resemble outdoor terrariums.

The orientation and exposure of a garden wall set the parameters of these niches, which are always unique. This is just what many adventuresome gardeners love, and we happily spend a lifetime discovering, adopting, and appreciating the plants that settle in among wall stones.

Low walls topped with flat, overhanging capstones can double as benches that blend into the landscape.

Scaling Stone Walls

A stone wall need not be long to work wonders in the garden, and you may find that the intermittent use of stacked stone works best if your yard is small. In addition to the height and breadth of the walls you hope to build, consider the size of the stone you will use. Walls built with large stones have a heavier presence than those made from smaller stones, so they appear more massive even when they are modest in height. Stone size is also relevant to the height of the wall. Walls less than 2 feet tall are easily built from small stones, but a wall that reaches 4 feet or higher must include numerous large stones to give it good stability. Tall walls also must be thick — usually at least 20 inches — while low ones will stand firm when the stone stacked is only 8 to 12 inches wide from front to back.

Batter and Pitch

"Batter" is the angle at which a wall slopes backward into the slope. It is sometimes called thrust. Both retaining walls and freestanding stone walls should have a batter that measures between 5 and 10 degrees (roughly the angle drawn by the hands on a clock that reads 12:02). In a retaining wall, the batter angle prevents the wall from being pushed to pieces by the pressure of the soil behind it. In a freestanding wall, both sides of the wall slant inward, toward the center top, so that the weight pushes in upon itself.

Setting stones at a slight backward pitch, so that they angle downward slightly from front to back, helps reinforce the batter while holding the stones firm when they are exposed to the force of water flowing over and through the wall.

When building small walls in informal areas, you can usually check the batter angle with your eyes.

A strong batter and wide tie stones make this curving wall stable. Even in winter, the wall retains its simple beauty.

Larger, more formal stone walls benefit from being checked often with a batter board. This is a board cut at exactly the angle you want that can be set on its end and used as a guide to keep the thrust consistent and true.

Straight Lines and Curves

A wall that is straight or only slightly bowed creates strong lines in a landscape. However, walls that curve are no more difficult to build, because, compared with the symmetry of bricks or cut stone blocks, the irregular shapes of most stacking stones make them easy to arrange in curves. The only special technique needed to build curving walls is to include very wide stones, called tie stones, in the most tightly curved sections of the wall.

End Stones and Capstones

Before you begin construction on a stone wall, it's a good idea to select two types of special stones you will need — end stones and capstones — and set them aside so they will be ready when you need them. The ends of a wall are usually the most vulnerable parts, so it's essential that the end stones be large, stable, and nearly square in shape. Large stones that fit together tightly are best, or you can place a very large, thick stone, planted on its end, as a pressure-resistant end stone. Large stones planted vertically are particularly useful where stone walls adjoin stone steps.

The capstones that will form the top of your wall should be as flat and uniform as possible, especially if you plan to sit on the wall or use it as a place for displaying plants grown in containers. On the other hand, if you want your wall to appear more formidable, jagged stones set on their ends along the top of the wall (which can be set in crevices within the top tier of stones) can be counted upon to deter passage by people. The top of a wall is also a good place to display personal treasure stones that are rich in fossils or dramatically marked with crystals.

Limestone blocks topped by thick, smooth, overhanging capstones (ABOVE) form an intermittent wall with plenty of elbowroom for roses.

Heavy stones top the wall that frames a sunken patio (ABOVE). Flat stone faces give the wall a smooth, well-crafted look.

Clearly intended to structure the garden, the trimmed foundation and capstones emphasize this mortared wall's formal style (RIGHT).

Retaining Walls

If your yard includes a prominent slope away from your house, you have an excellent site for a low retaining wall that accomplishes several goals. It will replace the slope with two tamer ones that are easier to cultivate and maintain. A stone foundation bed that is visually linked to your house's foundation also creates a frame that makes your house appear more settled in place. In the front yard, such a wall imparts a feeling of symmetrical balance and sets a neat, orderly mood.

When located in a side yard or backyard, a low retaining wall may be supremely practical. For example, a side yard that slopes down to a driveway or walkway benefits from leveling by making the traffic area less prone to flooding and erosion. In the backyard, a wall can create a platform for an elegant patio ensconced amid lush green plants.

Part of the beauty of this project is that it requires little in the way of site preparation beyond cutting into the slope to form a foundation for the wall. Then wall building can proceed as described on pages 112 and 113. You will probably need to add fill soil to the area to be retained by the wall; some of this soil

can come from the slope just below it. Additional topsoil will probably be needed, too, though it's important not to pile up too much soil against the foundation of your house. Never raise the level of a foundation bed to less than 6 inches from where siding begins, and preserve a slight grade away from your house so that rainwater will drain in the right direction. In high-rainfall areas, also consider including buried drainage pipes that run from the downspouts of your gutters, and then under the wall, ending at a place where the water can do no harm.

Sideways Slopes

In addition to having to rework the slope that runs perpendicular to your house, you may also be faced with a slope that runs across your yard, from one side to the other. Here you have a choice between having the top of your wall level, so that it echoes the lines of your house, or building the wall so that its top slopes with the fall of the land. Most people prefer the first option. If you are working with modest-sized stone, you can let the wall itself adjust to the crosswise slope. At the high end of the slope, the wall can melt into the soil, and you can turn the low end (where the wall itself is higher) into a focal point by adding a gate or arbor. With blockier stone, it is often more practical to "step down" the wall in strategic places, so that the top of the wall includes angular drops where a course of stone steps down to the one below it. Gracefully cascading evergreen shrubs, such as rockspray cotoneaster

Exuberantly flowering Siberian catmint is perfectly at home in the old-fashioned garden at the top of this low retaining wall near the front door.

Rough stone walls structure a hillside garden lush with peonies, creating a safe spot for a lawn and plantings of herbs.

(Cotoneaster horizontalis), creeping juniper *(Juniperus* species), or wintercreeper *(Euonymus fortunei),* can help soften the hard edges of these visual steps.

Panel Planting

Framing a foundation bed with a low wall creates new planting space, and it's up to you whether you grow a diversity of plants or fill the panels with low-maintenance ground covers, such as English ivy, pachysandra, or *Vinca minor.* Going with ground covers usually makes the space appear more expansive, which is an important asset to a small yard.

If you prefer more color, stick with low-growing plants that form soft mounds of fine-textured foliage, perhaps interspersed with little bulbs and dwarf annuals for additional seasonal color. Prime perenni-

als for this purpose include basket-of-gold, candytuft, dianthus, and creeping phlox. In summer, add ageratum, lobelia, petunia, sweet alyssum, and other mound-forming annuals to the mix.

Add a Tree

In places where a stone wall retains a foundation bed and the area in front of the wall is open lawn, consider planting a small ornamental tree a few feet out from the wall if you can do so without blocking the view from your windows. The upright form of the tree will provide visual contrast with the horizontal line of the wall, and it will make the wall appear a little softer, especially in winter. Good trees for this purpose include dwarf ornamental apricots, cherries, or crabapples; Japanese maples; or hardy deciduous magnolias. ■

A Working Garden Wall

The artistic possibilities of a sun-drenched retaining wall that faces the landscape head-on are so numerous that there is but one way to begin — by spending some time imagining and envisioning all that the scene can become. As a starting point, let's assume that you have decided on the site, so you know where the wall will stand. Now you must conjure up its role in the garden. Will it be a backdrop, a display place for plants, or both? How will you strike a balance between stone and plants, so that they flatter rather than obscure one another? What will the wall express about the place, the forces that shape it, and you as a gardener?

Ways to Fall

An expansive retaining wall strongly signals that there is a change in elevation, a fall. The height of the wall reflects the extent of the fall, but the way stones are stacked tells of its nature. Symmetrical placement of tight-fitting stones speaks of domestication, or close human management, which may be exactly what you want. However, if you look at how nature handles elevation changes, it's hard not to notice how horizontal shelves of stone alternate with tumbled pools of broken pieces. Perhaps this is why subtle patterns that emerge when horizontal courses are interrupted by large faces of stone often are so pleasing. They mimic the way stones arrange themselves when pulled down a slope by gravity and then scoured by water.

Our eyes always look for patterns, and we quickly zero in on the strong horizontal and vertical lines of a retaining wall. Things get even more interesting when the wall itself includes small trills of diagonal lines, such as you might create by placing three nearly identical stones in a diagonal pattern across three courses of stone. For reasons no artist, physicist, or mathematician has ever been able to explain, we are most interested (and satisfied) by odd numbers of roses in a vase or odd numbers of particularly eye-catching stones in a wall. So patterns drawn with texture or color that involve three, five, or seven stones usually work better than those in even numbers.

A curving wall retains every speck of improved soil in a bed teeming with Shasta daisies, centaurea, Oriental poppies, and other perennials.

Muting the Message

The type of stone you use and how you stack it tell your story of how the land fell the way it did, and then plants fill in the details. Your first major decision has to do with which voice speaks louder — that of the wall or that of the plants. Every inch of the wall that is clothed in foliage mutes the wall's message while introducing the element of time. A bare wall will tend to look new and fresh, while one colonized with plants appears much more ancient.

If you want to show off everything, leaving nothing out, the preferred strategy is to keep most of the wall clear by growing neat, mound-forming plants along the top of the wall and small dwarf species at its base. This can be a lot of fun, though the challenge of season-long appeal is as formidable as in any other type of gardening. Do keep in mind that long-lived perennials are best for the base of the wall, because annuals and other plants that require ongoing digging can compromise the stability of the wall. In sun, good choices for a wall base include miniature daffodils and other small, spring-flowering bulbs, which can be followed by daylilies, blazing star *(Liatris),* and late-blooming showy sedum *(Sedum spectabile).*

You will see more garden than wall if you emphasize cascading plants at the top of the wall, accompanied by foreground vines that thread their way upward. This approach is especially effective near the edges of the wall, where you probably want the stone to fade into a forest of foliage. For example, Boston ivy or Virginia creeper (both native *Parthenocissus* species) might dress the ends of the wall, with dramatic cascades of moss verbena or candytuft billowing down from the top.

Mixing Materials

Mixing various types and sizes of stone is the perfect way to turn a garden wall into a work of art. For example, combining rounded or only slightly faced stones with layers of angular sheets of shale or slate provides riveting contrast in texture and color. Or you can get more subtle highlights by setting glittery chunks of granite in a wall made primarily of limestone. The range of colors available in sandstone makes it extremely painterly, with patterns of color threaded through the wall in true tapestry style. ▪

Tree Wells of Stone

One of the most popular ways to use low stone walls, especially in small yards, is to put them to work masking or dressing the base of a large shade tree. This practice is both decorative and functional, because it creates a buffer zone around the base of the tree that anchors the tree in place while simplifying maintenance. Commonly called a tree well, a collar of stonework encircling a tree's trunk keeps the trunk safe from possible damage from mowers and string trimmers, and the interior of the well can be planted with ground covers or tough perennials to make it even more beautiful.

For the sake of the tree, it's important that the well be rather shallow, especially if you plan to add topsoil. The base of a tree and the topmost roots need to breathe, so take care to add no more than 6 inches of soil over the surface at the drip line (the point that marks the extent of the leafy canopy above) and taper the added topsoil to nothing as you get to the trunk. Because the base of a tree may be slightly higher than surrounding ground after a raised stone bed is filled with soil, the bed is typically deepest at the drip line and naturally comparatively shallow as it nears the trunk.

Of course, there is no rule that says that tree wells must be filled with soil and plants. A large tree trunk growing within the protection of a low dry-stacked wall is beautiful in itself, and the wall will naturally fill with leaves and mulch. In dry woods, trees often arise from clusters of stone, sometimes breaking apart large boulders as they grow. This is yet another natural arrangement you might mimic as you create a tree well in your landscape.

Shape Matters

Most tree wells are circular, mirroring the roundness of the tree's base. But tree wells also can be outlined as teardrops or crescents — an effective way to stabilize sloping ground while keeping the tree's shallow roots safe from erosion, or to showcase a group of small trees to create the effect of a grove. And if the low side of the tree well is deeper than the high side, you have an ideal planting spot for small companion shrubs that crave shade, such as azaleas and rhododendrons. Plants that thrive in relatively level and symmetrical circular tree wells include ferns, hostas, liriope, pulmonaria, sedum, and wood hyacinth, as well as vining ground covers such as English ivy and perennial vincas. For seasonal color, you can also plant tree wells with shade-tolerant annuals such as impatiens or torenia.

Avoiding Dry Wells

Even when a tree well is filled with rich, moisture-retentive soil, chronic dryness can be a problem because of the umbrella-like way that tree canopies capture and shed water. This problem is best solved by installing a soaker hose a few inches inside the stone well where it can be hidden from view by soil and mulch. Camouflage the female fitting at the end of the soaker hose by hiding it among stones on the back side of the well.

A low retaining wall around a tree protects the trunk from lawn-mower damage while providing a slightly raised planting bed for shade-loving plants such as impatiens.

Bulbs such as these tulips can provide a tree well with a splash of springtime color.

Creating a Tree Well

Choose stone that is native to your area, or of a type already used in your yard. As with all stone walls, it is essential to begin with a firm base of large, flat stones. Then you can switch to smaller stones before topping the wall with heavy stones to hold the structure together. Never use mortar in a tree well, because the growth of the tree and its surface roots will invariably cause the mortar to crack. With a dry-stacked wall, you can simply rearrange stones as needed to accommodate the changing size of the tree.

To avoid injuring shallow roots, excavate as little as possible when preparing the base for your tree well. As the tree and its roots will almost certainly continue to grow, allow a minimum of 2 feet of open space around the trunk, and stack stones around large protruding roots. If you are working on a slope, begin at the low side and slowly work upward, filling the well with well-tamped soil as the wall rises higher. In this situation, be sure to stack stones so that the wall pitches backward, into the slope. Don't be concerned that the pitch is noticeable, because tree wells that are acutely curved look even more dramatic when the wall tilts toward the upright tree. ■

Simple stones are ideal for edging a clean-swept garden of herbs, roses, and a few selected edibles and flowers.

Historical Herbs

More than any other plants, herbs foster close relationships with both our ancestors and the earth. Whether you use herbs for cooking, medicine, or just the pleasure of their invigorating aromas, these special plants often feel like mysterious gifts. It seems natural to provide herbs with living quarters of timeless stone.

Hardy herbs are often willing to grow in any spot that provides them with sun and good drainage. Yet the advantages of growing herbs in raised beds are numerous: Drainage is even better; plants are more accessible for planting, watching, and pinching; the soil warms a little earlier in spring; and you have complete control over the soil composition within the bed.

Marrying Herbs with Stone

The low walls that frame herb beds are built like other walls, with a few simplifications. In a stone-lined herb bed, no gravel is needed. Rather, rich yet gritty soil comes into direct contact with the stone walls that hold it in place, sometimes seeping out through the crevices.

Herbs are such congenial plants that it's best to keep them close at hand, so that you can quickly gather a few sprigs for cooking. Whenever possible, locate herb beds near outdoor living areas or adjacent to paved pathways. Herbs with aromatic foliage — such as basil, scented geraniums, and mints — will perfume the air if you gently swish your hand through the leaves. However, because herbs often attract bees and other buzzing insects, it is usually best to grow them at least a few yards from entryways.

Using stone rather than wood to contain herb beds gives you more freedom over shape. Circles, teardrops, or rounded triangles are possible, so there's no reason to limit yourself to graveyard rectangles. The height of the walls that enclose an herb bed should be at least 12 inches and can be as much as 24 inches if you prefer. The higher the walls, the more important it will be for them to pitch inward slightly so they will stand firm despite pressure from the soil within.

Creating Herbal Tapestries

I suppose it's possible to grow an herb garden with all green foliage, but the soft grays of rosemary and sages, the rich bronzes of 'Opal' basil or bronze fennel, and the bright chartreuse of golden thyme are but a few of the many choices you have for adding exciting color and texture to your collection of herbs. Also, think of how you can use herbs with surprising forms, such as upright chives or mounds of borage. To make sure all plants receive ample sun, locate tall species in the center or rear of the bed, with smaller plants in the foreground. Dwarf parsley is unsurpassed as an intermittent edging, particularly when interspersed with colorful, perky nasturtiums.

Historically, large herb gardens have often included accents such as sundials, gazing globes, statuary, or well-figured stones placed in strategic spots. Containers planted with herbs that tend to be invasive, such as mints, can be stationed nearby, or you might even use rubble stone to build a small cairn (circular mound of stone) to complete the scene. These and other accents introduce a human element to the herb garden, emphasizing the unique way that these special plants serve us by delighting our senses and promoting well-being.

Herbs for Walls and Crevices

You need not plant all of your herbs within your raised bed. Several varieties are equally happy scrambling over the top edges, nestling themselves into crevices between stones, or colonizing the base of the stone wall. Some species to try include creeping rosemary (*Rosmarinus officinalis* cultivars), sweet marjoram *(Origanum majorana)*, oregano *(Origanum* species), winter savory *(Satureja montana)*, and creeping thyme, like the *Thymus praecox* ssp. *arcticus* 'Albus' pictured here. ▪

A Grotto Wall

Gardeners often lament the presence of low, shady places in their property, but the presence of a stone wall changes everything. Chronic dampness becomes an asset when it fosters the proliferation of velvety mosses. Dimness creates cool pockets of space ideal for relaxing in hot weather. The heavy structure of the wall infuses the spot with the intimacy of a secret room, serene in mood and protected from the outside world.

In many landscapes, the area that best fits this description is found on the side of the house, though you might have a natural grotto in your backyard, too. Don't let this unique space go to waste; walling it in and furnishing it with a floor and ceiling leads to a dramatic transformation. In time, it may become your favorite place to refresh and restore yourself.

Conquering Chaos

The primary challenge in taming dark, dank areas is that they are naturally messy — slimy underfoot, often littered with plant debris, and frequently colonized by slugs and snails. To correct these defects, study ways you can enhance the floors and ceilings so that they will work well with the wall you plan to build.

For example, the floor should be as porous as possible, so that water drains away quickly rather than pooling up. A stone walkway that includes numerous wide crevices will do the trick, or you can substitute gravel. Where the floor meets the wall, it is a good idea to leave an open space covered with loosely stacked smooth stones, so that water that runs down the wall encounters a natural drain as soon as it reaches the level plane.

Overhead, you may find that thinning back tree branches improves both light and air circulation. Or, if the area gets too much harsh sun during part

Azaleas, heucheras, hostas, and other shade lovers grow
into a lush jungle above and in front of a fine-textured wall.

of the day, an open pergola type of ceiling covered
with vines will filter the light and accentuate the
intimate feeling of the space beneath it.

Reflective Walls

A stone wall in a close, shady place is best built of
small stone rather than stone that is massive and
blocky, which can overwhelm the scale of the outdoor room. Small stacking stone so well faced that it
is nearly rectangular is ideal for both practical and
aesthetic reasons. The numerous crevices help manage drainage water, and the fine detail in the texture
of the wall is reassuringly domestic.

Indoors, we naturally turn away from walls, con-
centrating instead on the centers of our rooms, but
the opposite reaction often takes place in an outdoor grotto type of room. Expect to be attracted by
the texture and life of a shady stone wall; you may
find that you even want to place seating so that it
faces the wall. This type of wall is also more
touchable than other stone features, particularly
when it seeps with moisture sufficient to support
mosses, little ferns, or other peculiar life forms. Take
care to place plants, containers, or other accents so
that they do not become barriers that make the
wall difficult to touch.

A Rock Roost

There is something about a low stone wall that invites children to climb and others to sit. If you have an area near your patio that you would like to partition from the space beyond it, or if you want to erect a similar barrier alongside a grassy spot that begs for structure, a freestanding wall built to be sat upon will divide and define the space while providing all-season seating. Because this type of wall is straight and topped by smooth, uniform capstones, it also has the formal demeanor necessary to win it a place in your front-yard landscape, perhaps where the walkway makes a sudden turn toward the door.

Unlike many of the other walls in this chapter, a sitting wall is typically freestanding, though you can also top a low retaining wall with level capstones to make it double as a bench. Height is critical, in that we expect sitting surfaces to be approximately 18 inches from the ground. Fortunately, walls built to this height are simple to construct using standard wall-building methods.

A sitting wall made of stone is usually thicker than a retaining wall, because it is comprised of two parallel stacks — front and back — that pitch slightly toward the center. As long as the front and back sides are securely stacked, any open space in the middle can be filled with rubble stone and gravel. To help the filler hold the sides firmly in place, be sure to pack it in well with a rebar stake, the same way you would pack gravel behind a retaining wall.

The Stone Duet

To make the sitting space as inviting as possible, you will probably want to buy cut stone for the capstones. As long as the capstones work well with the stacking

A lovely composition of stone, pot, ferns, and bronze-leaved heucheras invites close contact with a sittable stone wall.

The Question of Mortar

If the capstones you use are large and heavy, and if you are meticulous in stacking the wall so the capstones rest upon an absolutely level and secure surface, there may be no need to mortar them in place. However, mortar is usually used in this situation, both to secure the capstones and to provide the opportunity to adjust any small defects in the top of the wall.

Before mixing mortar according to package directions, lay the capstones over the wall and make any adjustments necessary to ensure firm placement. Then set them aside and mix only enough mortar for your needs. You can estimate by counting the number of corners on your capstones. Beneath each corner, about 2 inches in from the edges, you will use about 1 cup of mixed mortar. For a small wall, you can probably mix this amount in a plastic bucket. Be sure to wear heavy rubber gloves, because mortar is caustic.

Begin by dumping about a cup of mortar onto each place on the wall where the corners of the first capstone will rest. Then gently set it in place, but don't press on it yet. Deposit piles of mortar for the two adjoining capstones, set them in place, and then get out your carpenter's level and a rubber mallet. Place the level over the seam between two of the adjoining capstones, and gently press and tap on the capstones to make the surface even. Check the level from front to back, too, and then move on to the other seam between capstones. Follow this procedure until all capstones are in place. To give the mortar time to cure, do not allow anyone to sit on the wall for at least two days.

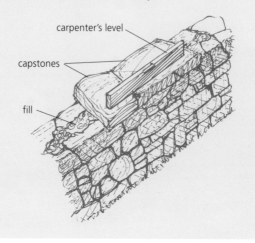

carpenter's level

capstones

fill

stone in terms of color and texture, feel free to use different stone for the capstones and for stacking — for instance, sandstone capstones with a limestone wall. Because cut stone is more costly than stacking stone, you may want to decide on the capstones first. Whether rectangular or square, capstones should form a sitting surface at least 12 inches deep. In addition, the capstones should form a small ledge that overhangs the wall below by at least ½ inch on all sides. This means that you can use relatively small stacking stone for the wall itself, though you will need a few large stones for the base course and the corners. As you choose and position stones, keep in mind that the area near the ground will be highly visible, but the top few inches of the wall will be hidden from view by the capstones.

Captive Fragrance

A little extra warmth helps bring out the fragrance of many of the plants treasured for their luscious aromas. By blocking the wind, a stone wall also can create an enclosure that captures the scents of the garden, especially in early evening, when many plants are at their fragrant best.

If you live in a cool climate, you will find that a stone wall facing south makes a big difference in how much of your plants' fragrance you get to enjoy. To pull off this feat, the wall needs to be high enough to

Who could resist a sitting area (ABOVE) where you rub elbows with lavender and press your feet into thyme?

Roses ramble at will over a roughly hewn stone wall (BELOW), which captures their heady fragrance.

serve as both a heat reservoir and a windbreak, which means it should be about 4 feet tall. Including stone walkways or landings near the wall will help capture even more warmth, though you will want to allow a broad planting space at the base of the wall to accommodate roses, honeysuckle, and other plants beloved for their perfumes.

Depending on the site, a wall designed to capture fragrance can be freestanding or can double as a retaining wall. In either case, bear in mind that the space behind the wall can also be used to grow fragrant plants that ramble over the top of the wall and into the interior garden. Because of their size and vigor, this is a good way to accommodate rambunctious vines such as sweet autumn clematis or wisteria. Or, if the area behind the wall is a shady woodland, fragrant woody plants such as Carolina allspice (*Calycanthus floridus)* or witch hazel (*Hamamelis* species) can form a fragrant curtain just beyond the garden wall.

Hidden Assets

Besides enhancing fragrance, a stalwart stone wall may give you a slight edge on winter hardiness, making it possible to successfully grow plants that are prone to cold injury when grown in an open garden. The microclimate created within the confines of a stone wall may be just the edge some plants need to survive in a borderline hardiness zone. For example, romantic English roses that normally struggle through Zone 5 winters may get precisely the protection they need from the wall, and the scenario would benefit gardenias in Zone 7.

In any climate, roses are often the cornerstone plants in fragrance gardens. They'll be flattered by ankle-deep carpets of sweet alyssum at their feet. Lavender or dianthus makes a fine companion for roses, too, and the frosty gray color of the foliage of both helps marry them to the texture of stone.

Fragrant upright annuals such as flowering tobacco (*Nicotiana* species) provide intoxicating evening fragrance, and it's always a good idea to keep pots of scented geraniums within touching distance in a fragrance garden. Other fine fragrance plants to grow in containers include spring-blooming hyacinths and summer-blooming heliotrope, which are best if you can place the pots near nose level.

Raising a Wall

Large landscapes can provide the scale to handle a tall wall made of large, blocky stone, but in smaller yards it is best to use smaller stones to help keep the wall in proper perspective with the rest of the landscape. The airy texture you get with small stones also flatters plants such as fragrant roses or ever-blooming honeysuckle that you can train to grow against the wall.

You may find that you would like the strong presence and privacy that a tall wall provides, but that one entirely made of stone is simply too expensive, or carries too much visual (and physical) weight. If you are afraid that a tall stone wall will overpower your landscape or your pocketbook, you always have the option of building a more modest-sized stone wall and topping it with a decorative fence made of wood or metal posts, which will lighten its appearance in the landscape. To solve a serious privacy problem, one excellent option is to add a wood, bamboo, or iron fence above a low stone wall.

Combining stone, wood, and plants in a wall gives an excellent opportunity to mix textures, shapes, and colors — from the formality of white pickets to the solidity of gray fieldstone to the exuberance of flowering vines. The time to plan this feature is before the wall is built, because the wood fence will need to be

attached to tall posts firmly set into the ground, usually with concrete footers. Once the posts are installed and the concrete has cured, you can build a stone wall between and around the posts. If the base of the posts is hidden from view by stone, the wood portion of the fence will appear to float atop the stone, lightening its appearance.

This combination of a low stone wall (FAR LEFT) topped by an elegant open fence and backed by small trees and shrubs defines a garden boundary without blocking the view.

In addition to creating privacy, a white wood fence (RIGHT) installed behind a stone wall suffuses the area with its brightness. The fence is softened by the variegated weigela atop the wall.

Consider Night Lights

After all the work of constructing and planting around it, you might not want to enjoy your new stone wall only during the day. You can easily dramatize a tall stone wall after dark by adding just the right outdoor lighting. Small spotlights, installed near the ground, softly illuminate the wall and the plants grown there; even outdoor-rated holiday garlands highlight a wall with a festive touch. Very strong lighting can make stone look somewhat garish, but low-wattage fixtures bring out the texture of stacked stone beautifully. Be sure to provide enough lighting along the paths that lead to your wall to make it easily accessible.

You should also consider how you can design your plantings and the stonework to make the lighting equipment and its accompanying wiring inconspicuous. Special weather-resistant wiring is needed for any type of outdoor lighting, but it is well worth the expense and effort to be able to enjoy this special kind of garden at night, when the fragrance of many flowers is strongest. ▪

Pillars and Thresholds

You can have the strong vertical presence of stone without the barrier of a stone wall by using stone to build pillars and special thresholds in the garden. These may be gateways to different gardens (with or without an actual gate) or simply stopping places where a garden begins, ends, or changes. You can build pillars alongside steps, at turning points in a pathway, or any place where you want to invoke a feeling that some kind of passage is taking place.

Pillars often come in pairs, but a single pillar that arises like a signpost in the landscape often needs no partner, especially if it is round rather than square in shape. Indeed, if you are working with rough stacking stone, it is often simpler to build pillars that are not precisely square. Strongly squared pillars are built primarily with large, squared-off cornerstones, which are expensive to buy and toilsome to trim. Rounded pillars, besides being easier to build, can be shaped to fit the site. For example, you can add a rounded oblong pillar that has the heavy presence of a wall, or you can accentuate the vertical plane by creating a pillar that is pyramidal in shape, narrowing as it rises.

Raising Pillars with Plants

Pillars at a garden's entryway that are less than waist high are inspirational because you can easily see over them to the garden beyond. And they are a little bit restful, too, since you can reach out to touch the solidity of stone, getting your bearings, or perhaps lean against a pillar — and even sit on it if it is the proper height — when you want to linger where the garden begins. You may feel, however, that the entrance to your garden needs a more definitive presence than a small pillar or set of pillars provides. One way to emphasize the vertical lines that structure a threshold, without smothering it with oversize stone pillars, is to plant strongly upright plants just beyond the pillars, so that the walls of the threshold are comprised of stone and plants, layered together. This is an ideal place to plant trees with attractive peeling bark, such as river birch *(Betula nigra)*; species that produce flowers and berries, such as hawthorns *(Crataegus* species); or muscular little redbuds *(Cercis canadensis).* In spaces too small to accommodate trees, birdhouses on tall posts or tall, columnar shrubs can serve the same purpose.

The visual details offered by fine-textured ferns make them an excellent choice for the sun-protected crevices in a shady wall.

Multidimensional Thresholds

The pillar or pillars that mark a threshold organize the garden by calling attention to its varying realms. Adding a small expanse of stone underfoot adds to the magic, so that you feel the passage on two sides. Ideally, threshold stones set into the ground should stretch from one side of the gateway to the other, emphasizing its width. Plan ahead for continuity by using the same type of stone in pillars as is used in the walking surface between them.

An arbor sturdy enough to support a climbing vine adds even more excitement to a threshold by giving it a ceiling. At least for a moment, you are sheltered as you pass from one part of the garden to another, and in that moment you can't help but experience a sensation of clarity, knowing that you are on the verge of entering a special place.

Perfect Pillars

With any type of pillar, it's crucial to place stone so that the pillar has a slight inward pitch, or batter. Unless the weight of the pillar pushes in upon itself, it will be highly prone to toppling over. Another way to build stability into a pillar is to include a large, heavy capstone at the top. A weighty capstone always gives a pillar a finished appearance and provides a perfect place for a large container or a piece of statuary.

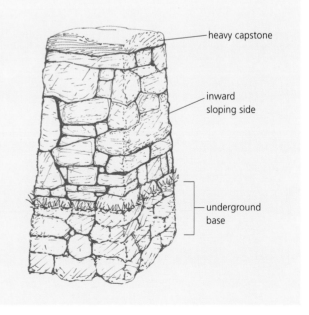

heavy capstone

inward sloping side

underground base

Plants for Stone Walls

Using a stone wall as your canvas, you have endless possibilities to display your artistry with plants. The usual site considerations — light, moisture, and temperature — tend to be exaggerated near a stone wall, so expect plenty of surprises as you experiment with plants to grow over, in, and at the base of your wall.

Softening the top of a wall with fine-textured plants that grow into cascading mounds always yields a graceful look. It is best not to allow the foliage to become so extensive that it hides the wall from view and eliminates the contrast of plant on stone. Exemplary flowering plants such as basket-of-gold, dianthus, and candytuft are perfect for this job, and they always appreciate the great drainage provided by planting pockets just behind a wall's top edge.

Moisture is the key to growing plants in wall crevices. Damp walls easily support ferns and mosses, but walls that bake in the sun require drought-resistant sedums. The base of a wall is a treasure niche that can be filled with an endless array of beautiful plants. Other possibilities are listed at the end of chapter 5, under "Plants for Rock Gardens." If the wall faces north or east, however, it's hard to go wrong with small woodland plants that are native to your area.

Basket-of-Gold (*Aurinia saxatilis*)

Growing only 8 inches tall but more than 12 inches wide, basket-of-gold makes a bold splash in spring, when the mounds of gray-green foliage are covered with tiny yellow blossoms. Adapted in Zones 4 to 8, this perennial makes exuberant new growth in spring and blooms early. A resolute sun lover, basket-of-gold is best trimmed back to half its size after the flowers fade. 'Compacta' (shown here) is a particularly good wall plant.

Alpine Clematis (*Clematis alpina*)

If the back of your stone wall rests in cool shade but the front of it gets at least five hours of sun, you have a sweet spot for alpine clematis. This gentle vine produces nodding blue, pink, or purple flowers in early summer that are smaller and very different in shape from the large-flowered clematis typically grown on trellises. Adapted in Zones 6 to 9, alpine clematis requires a pocket of fertile, near neutral soil, and benefits from regular feeding. Prune after the flowers fade, as this species blooms on the previous year's growth.

Ice Plant *(Delosperma* species*)*

These low-growing succulents are usually evergreen and so drought tolerant that they easily adapt to life in wall crevices that bake in the sun. Bright pink and long-flowering, *D. cooperi* (shown here) is rather warm natured and best grown in Zones 8 to 10. It grows 2 inches tall and 24 or more inches wide. More cold-tolerant ice plants include *D. floribundum* 'Starburst', with lilac-pink flowers, and yellow-flowered *D. congestrum* 'Gold Nugget', both hardy to Zone 4. All ice plants need very well-drained, gritty soil.

Dianthus *(Dianthus gratianopolitanus)*

Of all the varied dianthus available, this fragrant species is the first to try as a complement to a stone wall. 'Petite' is a particularly compact cultivar, at 3 to 4 inches tall. The gray-green, grassy foliage is beautiful even when the plants are not in flower. The spreading mats thin out somewhat in late summer but are fully recovered by late winter. It is easily grown in Zones 4 to 9.

Hosta *(Hosta* species and cultivars*)*

When in doubt about what to plant at the base of a shady wall, try hostas. These shade-tolerant beauties are famous for their foliage, which can be green, blue-green, variegated, or chartreuse. The foliage persists from spring to late fall, with flowering primarily in early summer. Growing and collecting hostas, which are adapted in Zones 3 to 8, often begins as a passion and soon becomes an addiction.

Candytuft *(Iberis sempervirens)*

This dainty perennial is evergreen in Zones 7 to 9 and withstands winter to Zone 5. It develops a cascading habit when planted atop a wall, or it will hug the ground when grown as an edging. The pure whiteness of candytuft blooms is dazzling. Older strains bloom only in spring, but reblooming cultivars, including 'Autumn Snow', stage a repeat performance in the fall.

Sweet Potato Vine *(Ipomoea batatas)*

In the few years that they have been available to gardeners, ornamental sweet potato vines have become mainstays in containers. *Ipomoea* is also an ideal vine to spill over a sunny wall, growing into a lush cascade of foliage. These plants must be treated as annuals, as vines die at the first hint of frost, and you will need to start with new purchased plants each spring. Look for cultivars with chartreuse or nearly black foliage for a touch of drama in your garden.

Creeping Phlox *(Phlox subulata)*

Tough and reliable, creeping phlox can be counted on to paint the garden in Easter-egg colors in mid-spring. Adapted in Zones 3 to 8, creeping phlox needs sun and winter moisture but asks for little in terms of soil. As long as walls are not more than 10 to 12 inches thick, plants often can be grown in roomy crevices. Phlox always thrives when allowed to dance over the top of a wall, or, with enough sun, you can let it fill low crevices and spread into walking surfaces.

Rock Soapwort *(Saponaria ocymoides)*

Easy to grow in wide wall crevices or atop a sunny stone wall, rock soapwort never fails to cover itself with tiny, brilliant pink flowers in late spring and early summer. Adapted in Zones 4 to 8, this herbaceous perennial often retains some green leaves in mild winter areas. Any well-drained soil with a near neutral pH will please rock soapwort, which benefits from shearing back in midsummer, after the flowers fade. Superior named varieties and hybrids grow only 3 inches tall and spread into 12-inch-wide bushy mounds.

Sedum *(Sedum species)*

Any sedum that grows less than 10 inches tall is worth trying on or in a stone wall. 'Vera Jameson' (shown here) has purple-pink leaves and soft pink flowers that bloom in late summer and early fall. Daintier kamchatka stonecrop *(S. kamtschaticum)* (shown on page 159) hugs stone like a deep carpet and blooms in summer. Mix these sedums with *S. spurium* (shown on page 77). All of these sedums are adapted in Zones 4 to 9.

Verbena (*Verbena* hybrids)

Verbenas come in many packages, but there have never been verbenas better for spilling over sunny walls than the new 'Tapien' verbenas (shown here), which resemble old-fashioned moss verbenas in their low, trailing growth habit. Colors include soft pink, salmon, and deep blue-violet. Tender perennials hardy only to about 15°F, these plants are best handled as annuals. Should they become ragged in midsummer, simply shear them back to half their size. Regular fertilizer boosts the flower potential of these verbenas.

Ferns (numerous species)

To mimic the way plants and stones work together in moist, shady woods, adopt ferns. Many species, such as the ostrich fern *(Matteuccia struthiopteris* var. *pennsylvanica)* shown here, thrive in a moist, shady nook at the base of a wall, and crevices in a wall's lower portions often stay damp enough to keep ferns happy. Give ferns plenty of water to help them get established, and they will stay with you forever. For help in selecting the right species for your location, inquire at a local wildflower nursery.

Moss (numerous species)

The best way to get moss to grow in and around a stone wall is to "seed" the wall with weathered stones that already have been colonized by wild mosses. Mosses grow in organic matter that accumulates in crevices and fissures, so newly cut stone will not support moss. Moss also needs moisture, so it grows best in walls near water gardens or in naturally damp spots. To colonize a hospitable wall with moss, poke plugs gathered from local woods into crevices in fall or spring, and be patient.

CHAPTER 5

ROCK GARDENING WITH STONE

Walls are walls and steps are steps, but a rock garden is a *garden* — a special place where plants are the main feature, yet stone sets the stage. The character of your rock garden will be strongly

influenced by your climate and by the site in which the rock garden is placed, but one outcome is certain: You will create a special habitat for plants that is far different from all the other parts of your landscape.

A rock garden is all about habitat — a distinct ecological niche created by combining stone, custom-blended soil, and plants that thrive in the special setting created in the process.

The Heart of Rock Gardening

Historically, the preferred plants for rock gardens are true alpines — small, rugged plants found growing in high elevations, such as the Swiss Alps. Coaxing these plants to grow in a warm climate at low elevations, however, is often difficult, so it is completely acceptable to substitute other plants, better adapted to your climate, as long as they are petite. Most rock-garden plants should be small of leaf, small of stature, and tight in growth habit. The idea is to mimic the natural stunted effect of life on a windswept mountain peak.

Miniature mountains are the classic models for rock gardens, but there are many other ways to create gardens amid stone. If your yard includes a natural rock outcropping, you can enrich the space among boulders by adding as much stone as is needed to create planting pockets for plants, and then add what's called a scree garden at the base. If neatness is your nature, a rockery designed in symmetrical steps may be the rock garden of your dreams. In a woodland setting, the rock garden can become a private sanctuary, where lush plants and stone are unified as one.

Although stone is a prominent presence in a rock garden, this is really a place that features plants. As a rule of thumb, the visible surface of a mature rock garden should be about two-thirds plants and one-third stone. Yet the rock garden also should look

Smooth rock outcroppings provide a place for sedums, achillea, astilbe, foxglove, lady's mantle, and other bulbs and perennials.

good naked; in winter, its lines and contours are all you are likely to see.

Because most rock gardens bake in the sun, it is seldom good to have them facing south or west. A cooler orientation toward north or east is best, except for rock gardens in shade. Especially in warm climates, rock gardens that receive at least a half day of shade tend to flourish, particularly when they are shaded during the hottest part of the afternoon.

When planning a rock garden, keep one thing in mind: As with all special gardens, it is wise to start small. Rock gardens must almost always be tended by hand, without help of mowers, string trimmers, or sometimes even rakes. You will almost certainly enjoy a small, carefully tended rock garden more than one that demands too much time and energy.

The Wisest Rocks

You can use any type of stone in a rock garden, though it's difficult to make smooth, unweathered cut stone look natural. Weathered stone that includes numerous fissures and crevices is best; it will look natural, and you can use its small nooks and crannies as planting pockets for tiny plants. Again, it's best to work with stone that matches the type used in other parts of your landscape.

The hardness of the stone you are using will affect its porosity. For example, sandstone is quite porous and actually absorbs water, which plants may eventually use. So the planting pockets and crevices can be small because of the stone's water-retention ability. In comparison, extremely dense basalt and granite are impervious to moisture, so your plants must take up all the water they need from the soil. This means that their roots will need deeper, roomier quarters.

The garden in the photos above makes use of both planting pockets filled with shrubs, perennials, and bulbs (TOP) as well as the exposed boulder itself (BOTTOM), where only a little soil is needed to support carpets of low-growing sedums.

Building a Rock Garden

Regardless of site and style, creation of a rock garden proceeds in logical steps. If you are working on a level site, install large boulders first. This usually requires substantial digging. Next, create the foundation for your rock garden, which may involve excavating existing soil to a depth of 12 inches or more and substituting a gritty soil mixture that will give the superior drainage required by most rock-garden plants. Because the foundation depth needed varies with the type of rock garden you are making, specific details on what should lie beneath mounded, scree, or woodland rock gardens are given later in this chapter.

If the site is a sloping one, it is generally best to begin at the bottom and work upward when placing stones. Also, strive to tilt stones backward a tiny bit, so that water will run back toward the slope, furnishing moisture for the plants that grow among the stones. Carefully bed each stone individually, planting it to at least half its depth, and jump on it to make sure it is firmly settled in place. Bear in mind that you will be using the largest stone surfaces as places to stand or squat as you tend your plants, so later on, when your garden matures, you'll appreciate strategically placed stones with flat upper surfaces.

Descending Order of Size

As gardeners, we are accustomed to planting tall, upright plants as backdrops, with shorter ones in front so that all can be seen to maximum advantage. The opposite approach is usually taken with rock

Carefully placed and planted stones help channel water toward plant roots (LEFT).

Exuberantly blossoming peonies anchor the bottom of a hillside rock garden (RIGHT).

gardens, however, where it's better to mimic the way plant size naturally decreases as one moves higher up a mountain. Lush, thick plants with large leaves are therefore traditionally limited to the lowest edges of rock gardens, with plants becoming smaller as elevation increases.

Unfortunately, this "tiny-at-the-top" principle won't work in all situations, especially in small gardens in tight quarters. Instead of having large plants hide smaller ones from view, the typical solution is to forego large plants completely and have all the species in a small garden be little ones.

As you place stones and create planting pockets in your rock garden, allow some broad spaces for plants that spread and smaller pockets for upright plants, such as small bulbs, that you will plant in

Underground Connections

When arranging stones for a rock garden, it's helpful to imagine that all of the stones are somehow connected underground. Use this trick to help keep natural fissures aligned and to pinpoint spots where you think stone should naturally bump up to the surface. ■

clusters. Rock gardens provide an unusual opportunity to use plants that spread aggressively, because you can use stone to restrain them from wandering where they are not wanted. Two popular rock-garden plants, rock cress (*Arabis* species) and carpet bugle (also known as bugleweed; *Ajuga reptans*), are good examples of spreaders that are easily kept in check by barriers of stone.

Rock Gardening Basics

Most rock-garden plants are well pleased with a three-part mixture of good topsoil, soft humus (compost, leaf mold, or peat moss), and sharp sand. It's wise to seek out the best ingredients, blend several batches in a wheelbarrow, and store the mixture in sealed pails until you are ready to use it.

On the other hand, rock gardening always involves a certain amount of tinkering with soil mixes when a plant does not appear satisfied. For example, most rock-garden plants prefer a slightly acidic pH, between 6.0 and 7.0. Because of their acidity, both leaf mold and peat moss are good sources of organic matter when you are growing woodland wildflowers, which often need slightly acidic conditions. Similarly, you may wish to boost soil acidity with these materials when the primary stone in your rock garden is soft limestone, which leaches its own steady supply of lime.

The soil mixture described here is very low in nutrients, which is acceptable to many rock-garden plants but inadequate for others. Historically, rock gardeners have used pulverized dried manure as a modest, slow-release source of nitrogen, along with bonemeal for slow-release phosphorus. Manure varies in its nutrient content, however, and often contains weed seeds. Concerns over mad cow disease have also made many gardeners give up bonemeal altogether. I think it is better to amend soil with a packaged all-purpose organic plant food with a low analysis, such as one made from fish, kelp, alfalfa meal, and a range of other organic ingredients.

Rock-garden plants such as daphne thrive in gritty soil with dry conditions at the surface, compliments of gravel mulch.

The widely varied leaf and flower colors of sedums (here, *S. sieboldii*) often change with the seasons.

Rock-garden plants usually respond badly to over-feeding; they thrive on some degree of adversity. A rich soil mix can make a naturally tight plant become weak and floppy or rob a perennial flower of its determination to bloom. Starvation is not pretty, either, so closely watch your plants to know which need more or less nutrition and which are perfectly satisfied.

Maintenance and Care

The same care required in other gardens — weeding, watering, feeding, and winter protection — applies to rock gardens as well. Patrol for weeds early and often, and pull them out by hand when the soil is wet. How you supply water depends on its availability. Most rock-garden plants are water misers by nature, but there will be times when they will beg for moisture. From an environmental point of view, the wisest way to provide water is through an efficient drip system installed belowground at the time the garden is made. This is so easy to do nowadays, either with kits or with buried soaker hoses, that there is little excuse for not giving it serious consideration.

Plant High, Mulch Dry

To give plants the best possible start in a rock garden, water them well before slipping them out of their containers, and then set them high, so that the top half inch of roots and container soil is exposed above the soil's surface. Water well to settle the plant in place, and then mulch with a scant 1 inch of clean pebbles or gravel. This procedure will provide the roots with the moisture they need but give the aboveground plant parts a dry environment, limiting pesky problems with mildew and other fungal diseases. ■

Occasional aboveground watering with a hose or sprinkler is fine, but many rock-garden plants abhor damp conditions at the surface. The goal is to get water deep between the rocks, where it is most needed. This kind of watering is best done in dry and windy conditions, so the leaves will dry off quickly.

As plants fade at the end of the season, clip away dead foliage that may harbor insects or diseases. If you live where winters are mild (Zones 7 to 9), fall is a good time to top-dress plants with a little organic fertilizer mixed with sand, because many rock garden plants will remain green through winter, and bulbs begin growing roots by Thanksgiving. Or you can wait until spring, the preferred time for feeding rock-garden plants in cold-winter climates. In all areas, as autumn leaves flutter to the ground, it is essential to remove debris to keep it from blocking light to plants and mosses. A small child's rake is useful for this job, or you can use a leaf blower.

Where winters are very cold (Zones 3 to 5), mulch over the rock garden with several inches of straw after you've cleaned up the debris in late fall. Because a rock garden protrudes above the surface, it is more prone to heaving. Gather up this blanket of insulating mulch as soon as the snow disappears in early spring, then top-dress plants lightly with a mixture of dry organic fertilizer and sand. Spring rains will melt it into the soil below, ready to be used by plants as they rise up with their spring growth spurt.

The cut stone dividers in this scree garden restrain the spread of plants such as ajuga, euphorbia, and sedums.

A Scree Garden

In nature, a scree is an area at the base of a rocky cliff or mountain where small pieces of broken rock accumulate. The rocks break as they fall, and then water rushing down the mountain pulverizes them more, so that the scree becomes a colony of stones of mixed sizes, with a deep underlying layer of gravel-sized stone. A scree is often quite deep, because before the place was filled with broken rock, it was most likely a pool or pit carved out by falling water.

Replicating a scree in your landscape is a beautiful way to make the most of a cliff base or any dry, open area punctuated by natural stone. A scree garden can be a continuation of another rock garden, or it can exist on its own. To make it look natural, shape your scree into an irregular fan, or let it curve as though it were shaped by water.

Shade is an unwelcome feature and, in fact, a scree garden looks best when it appears in a windswept, inhospitable site. A true scree typically has a back and a front, with large stones used to structure the back, giving way to rubble and small pebbles in the front. However, framing a scree garden with stone gives it definition, making it appear less wild.

Drainage is nothing short of fantastic in a scree garden, since it is basically gravel with just enough soil introduced to support plants. Plants that grow in scree are a special group able to thrive in this niche with the help of very deep, extensive roots. Because available nutrients are scant, these plants are accustomed to struggle, and giving them too much rich soil and water can interfere with their natural growth habits.

Creating a Scree

One of the fine distinctions of a scree garden is its depth. Whereas many rock gardens may be built atop the surface, for a scree it is necessary to modify the soil to a depth of 18 inches, or even deeper if the site does not slope sufficiently to promote fast drainage. Remove all of the soil and line the bottom of the area with a few inches of rubble stone and coarse gravel. For better drainage, you can also cut grooves into the base of the site to capture water and carry it away.

The soil for a scree garden contains more grit or gravel than the normal rock garden mix. About half of the mix should be an equal blend of soil and organic matter (leaf mold, compost, or peat moss); the rest is pure rock. You can choose rock chips, gravel, pebbles, coarse sand, or a mixture. A tool called a mattock is easier to use in a scree mix than a spade, which dulls quickly in rocky soil. Also, the long tines of a cultivator (also called a pronged hoe) do a better job of smoothing and shaping scree mix than the short tines of a regular garden rake.

To allow for settling, pile the mix at least 2 inches higher than nearby surfaces; wait a week or more for the mixture to settle before setting out plants. If you are placing larger stones within the scree garden, be prepared to use a number of small stones to help hold larger ones in place. Until it is well settled, scree mix alone is too unstable to hold large rocks.

Magical Moraines

Moraines are deposits of rock and soil left behind by glaciers, which create a habitat very similar to a scree, but usually without a host mountain and with the addition of water that frequently filters through the soil mixture. A water supply can come from irrigation pipes just under the surface or from an outlet that creates a gentle soaking flow. Moraines support plants found growing wild alongside rocky streams, and they often satisfy finicky plants that need more water than is available in a scree, or better drainage than is afforded by normal rock-garden conditions.

Repeat What Works

The principle of repetition works very well in scree gardens, because it mimics the type of ecosystem that would evolve in a natural scree site. As a starting point, allow one or two types of plants to predominate, planted in meandering drifts or intermittent colonies. In this way, you might use a scree garden to showcase a collection of sedums and sempervivums, which almost always thrive in scree conditions. In very arid climates, a scree makes a fine habitat for cacti as well. ■

A Stepped Rockery

In most rock gardens, extreme care is taken to situate stones so that they look as if they were planted by nature. A stepped rockery takes a different approach, bringing discipline to a site by creating symmetrical terraces, or steps, that include wide planting spaces behind them. This is the most formal of rock-garden designs. It is well suited to homes with classical architecture and to gardeners and others who like a strong dose of orderliness, indoors or out.

The same organization defined by the stone in a stepped rockery is reflected in the choice and placement of plants within the beds. In most cases, each step is used as a bed for an individual species, or perhaps two that grow together companionably and follow each other in seasonal order, such as spring-flowering daffodils or tulips partnered with summer-blooming daylilies.

Gardeners who enjoy small collections of plants such as iris, daylilies, lilies, or peonies are often well pleased with stepped rockeries. The stairstep design displays each beloved plant in all its glory, and the lines of stone around each bed serve as visual frames.

In the interest of unity, a single type of edging plant may be tucked into each of the steps — for example, perennial candytuft or dwarf annuals such as sweet alyssum or edging lobelia. The edging need not be planted in a continuous line, and in fact it has a softer effect if small, fine-textured plants appear as intermittent lace among the stones.

To create a stepped rockery, begin by stripping off the surface vegetation on the entire site. A sharp, flat-bladed spade works well for this job. Next, cultivate the space to a depth of 4 to 6 inches.

As with steps, start at the bottom and work your way upward, and as with a wall, begin at the corners and work your way inward. Excavate to form a flat, even foundation for the lowest bed, setting the soil aside in wheelbarrows, if necessary. Set stones as for a wall, with large heavy stones on the bottom and flat, tightly fitted ones along the top.

As you proceed upward, place broad boards or scrap plywood over the just-completed bed to protect it. Wait until the stonework is finished to modify the soil within the beds and set out plants.

Lavish Ledges

A less formal version of a stepped rockery is a ledge garden, in which stone is used to structure a modest slope into horizontal shelves, which may be far from parallel or symmetrical. Like a stepped rockery, a ledge garden includes plenty of planting space behind each tier of stone, with soil mixtures in those pockets varied as needed to support different plants. Rather than being limited to rock-garden plants, a ledge garden is almost like a wildflower meadow structured with stone. Bright-blooming prairie plants such as coreopsis and purple coneflower (*Echinacea purpurea*) can bring a ledge garden to life in grand style, often in the company of numerous spring-flowering bulbs, followed by catmints (*Nepeta* species).

The main requirements for a stepped rockery are a moderate slope and a good supply of large flat stones. It is best to begin this project on paper, using the same procedure for measuring the rise and run of a slope described for step construction on page 83. Indeed, building a stepped rockery is similar to building steps, with two distinct differences. First, the capstones in a stepped rockery need to tilt backward slightly, toward the planting beds, so that rainwater is channeled toward the plants at the rear of each step rather than being directed to dump into the lower tier in great sheets. Site preparation differs, too, because the areas between steps in a stepped rockery are destined for cultivation rather than serving as foundation for additional stone.

This natural ledge is evolving into an informal, stepped-rockery–style garden with iris, daylilies, and honeysuckle growing in its cracks.

Mountain in Miniature

How can you create a rock garden that resembles a miniature mountain and make it look as though it belongs in the city, the suburbs, or a spot of open countryside? This is a classic challenge for rock gardeners. Few of us have the space to implement the preferred cure, which is to locate the rock garden after a turn in a path, set off on its own behind a grove of trees. In yards that are measured in feet rather than acres, we must use other tricks to make a little mountain appear to fit in on the right scale.

One excellent approach is to have only half a mountain backed by a fence, so that the mountain appears to continue beyond the fence unseen. By making use of a plain structured backdrop such as a wood fence, you may be surprised what you can do with a partial mountain in a narrow side yard, or tucked into the corner of your front yard or backyard.

You also can separate the space dedicated to a miniature mountain with an evergreen hedge, slightly higher than the garden itself, so that it must be discovered in its special place in the landscape. The great advantage of separating a rock garden in this way is that the diminutive delights to be found there do not have to compete with the more arresting appearance of lush petunias or geraniums growing in pots on your patio.

Anchoring a mountain-style rock garden with a water feature has the added advantage of simulating additional height. When a Lilliputian mountain gives way to water — or even a low valley dug out

Evergreen shrubs hold court year-round, as an edging of posts and river stones separates rock garden from lawn.

and lined with a wash of rounded river stones — the elevation at the surface is lower, which makes the stonework behind it appear a little more massive.

A terraced rock garden shelters lavender, bleeding heart, and daisies.

Delightful Details

The smaller the size of a freestanding rock garden, the more important it is to attend to details of texture, form, and dramatic tension. To make the garden look as though it belongs, pay close attention to how the largest stones relate to one another. Envision the underground connections discussed on page 137, and make sure that layers or natural fissures in stones parallel one another. If you can obtain rounded stones with numerous pocks or bubbles on one side, use them in the foreground, where they will be seen to maximum advantage.

To make your mountain more fun, exploit every square inch by including small overhangs and dark openings you might think of as frog caves, dry water runs curving around the side of the mount, and perhaps a gravel or stone landing that connects to a walkway. Also, plan for some type of seating, because you will want to sit back and enjoy your creation.

Seasonal Selections

The palette of alpine and other rock garden plants is rich in species that bloom in spring, such as rock cresses, primulas, and small spring-flowering bulbs. Indeed, true alpines come from climates where summer is brief, so it's no wonder that spring is their strongest season.

To keep a miniature mountain alluring through summer's second half, include plants with interesting, long-lasting foliage, such as sedums, sempervivums, and saxifrages, along with species that wait until sum-

mer or fall to bloom. Heathers (*Calluna vulgaris),* penstemons (*Penstemon* species), and little veronicas (*Veronica* species) will keep a rock garden well supplied with color through the summer months.

Remember, too, that you can make changes as you see the need, which often happens once plants become established and reveal their mature textures and forms. A plant that's too upright near the summit may look unkempt or downright silly, and you never know when a spreading plant will grow so well that it hides too much stone from view. A rock garden that gets lost in foliage loses the heaviness it needs to remind us of the mountain image, the aspect of the garden that symbolizes stability and permanence. So, instead of placing and nurturing plants that overtake the scene, strive for an organized collection of little gems, each of which adds sparkle to the mount with its color and form.

Stone Bowls

You can use fine-textured annuals grown in containers to add seasonal color to the scene, but it's important to make sure that they match their surroundings. Low stone bowls planted with sweet alyssum or moss verbena work well, but this is not a good place for upright pedestal-style containers or plants with large leaves. In comparison, a broken clay pot, half buried in pebbles with moss rose (portulaca) emerging from its mouth would look much more at home. ■

Stone in Japanese Style

Gardeners in China and Japan have used stone as central garden elements for thousands of years. When first encountered by Europeans, the rock gardens of China seemed wildly informal, so different were they from the straight lines and balance of gardens at home. Asian gardens offered something very new yet very old — an undeniable naturalism — that Europeans eagerly sought to emulate. Here in America, we are still pursuing this quest, often by following the principles of garden harmony and symbolism refined by the gardeners of Japan.

Each of several defined types of Japanese gardens, including the tea garden, the stroll garden, and the dry landscape garden, has its own distinctive features and purpose. I urge you to study any specific type of garden you want to create, as well as the place where the garden will exist. Here I will touch on the most important features in the Japanese garden, beginning with the timeless role of stone.

Eternally Changing Stone

In Japanese philosophy, nature is constantly teaching us two fundamental things: The universe is eternal, and it is always changing. Stones that mimic mountains, water that shimmers or flows with life, and sky that goes on forever set the framework for a Japanese garden that communicates these lessons. At its best, a Japanese garden is an artistic rendering of these natural elements, undergirded with a serenity that soothes the spirit.

Simplicity is a great guideline to keep in mind when dreaming up plans for a Japanese garden, which can be built around a few select stones, a small water feature, and a carefully chosen palette of plants. Because the stones will represent the eternal aspect of nature, their selection and placement is a logical place to begin. Japanese gardens are all about encounters in which the harmony of nature is mirrored back and forth between the human and what he or she sees, hears, smells, touches, and perceives on a spiritual level.

This being the case, I suggest spending some time imagining how you will encounter the stone in a garden. Will you look at it, walk around it, stand or sit on it, or let it lead your footsteps? Once you know where and how you will use stone, the rest of the garden can be orchestrated to make the scene feel harmonious and tranquil.

The next most important element, water, can be brought to the garden through either symbolic stone or actual water. In dry gardens, often called Zen gardens, raked, light-colored gravel is used to simulate the presence of water. However, gardeners often like the dynamic presence of the real thing, which can be introduced via a small basin or a pond large enough to accommodate a few colorful fish. Chapter 6 includes a number of ways to bring water to the garden that are consistent with Japanese style.

The simple harmony between natural and symbolic elements in a Japanese garden (LEFT) is the essence of serenity.

An intentional arrangement of different types of stone of similar size (ABOVE RIGHT) exemplifies nature's diversity.

Symbolic Plants

Part of the magic of a Japanese garden lies in the way it idealizes nature rather than replicating it. Instead of the huge array of plants you might find in a wild area near your home, plants in the Japanese garden are carefully chosen for their ability to symbolize the natural flow of the seasons. Dwarf pines and other evergreens are often prominent because they bring constancy to the garden, and some Japanese gardens exclude all flowers and deciduous plants in the interest of clarity.

Gardeners who are interested in drama and color will want to include at least some of the most classic plants when creating this style of garden. To celebrate spring, we can add flowering cherries or plums, which can be as dwarf as needed to fit the scale of any garden, perhaps with the companionship

of some small azaleas. Along the water's edge, we might find the perfect spot for upright iris. Wherever they seem to fit, Japanese maples or clumps of bamboo always serve to exemplify the style that we think of as distinctively Japanese, as does the graceful sway of a willow. Finally, we might decide to raise the garden's color level in the fall with bright golden chrysanthemums.

If you are a collector at heart, there is one perfect way to accommodate this passion within the Asian style — bonsai. Meticulously tended plants grown in miniature, whether in containers or in the ground, are the way to go if you love to collect as much as you love the serenity of an Asian garden. Bonsai are also ideal companions for the exploration of size and scale that is at the heart of rock gardening.

The elegant red-leaved maple in this Japanese garden (LEFT) becomes even more vivid in the fall.

Brassy gold and blood red chrysanthemums (ABOVE) are classics of the Japanese garden in fall.

Once plants become established in crevices, their foliage and roots usually can hold on to all the organic matter they require.

Blended Boulders

Creating a garden in a site that is dominated by large boulders requires an attitude of acceptance. The site has provided you with a dramatic natural sculpture, so the garden you create will become its frame — or, stated more poetically, the enhanced fantasy world born of your creative endeavors.

It's clear from the outset that the boulders are in charge of things, so you will work with and around them. This can be a tricky business, because your eyes may be so accustomed to seeing how nature arranges stones that any big changes you make run the risk of appearing awkward or contrived. It's hard to go wrong if you are meticulous in allowing the boulders and companion stones to work together harmoniously. If you are lucky enough to be working among sedimentary rock in which the layers, or strata, are clearly visible, you can use those lines (which should go in the same direction) to structure the garden as a whole.

Work around one, two, or three key stones, which are the largest ones in your composition. Look for natural cups and fissures where soil can be brought in to create planting sites for low, creeping plants that will form living blankets on or among the stones. Sedums and small creeping thymes are ideal for this job, or you can use mosses, ferns, or ivies if the site is shady. Don't miss the opportunity to unify big boulders with more domesticated sections of your landscape by repeating plants grown atop boulders at the base of the outcrop, so that they appear to have colonized and spread via the same natural forces that shaped the boulders. As plantings stretch out into the foreground, mulch around them with rock chips or gravel that matches the type of stone in the outcrop.

Basking among Boulders

Where boulders predominate, you will need to fit in walkways, steps, and sitting areas wherever you can. In very rocky yards, many gardeners build decks atop the boulders to create a flat place to enjoy their handiwork, sometimes sculpting the edges of decks so that they are molded into the rock. Large, upright boulders also impart a welcome sense of enclosure when they are used as walls for sitting areas. It's important to downplay man-made structures, however, particularly from the vantage point from which the outcrop garden will be viewed. Hiding fences and buildings from view with shrubs and trees lets the natural beauty of the scene remain uncompromised. Or you can arrange seating so that the outcrop forms a protected backdrop for the rest of the landscape.

If you need to add stone to make your garden more accessible or to improve structure or symmetry, look for stone that matches the existing boulders in terms of color and texture. This is usually not difficult, since the environment of which your yard is a part likely has lots of loose stone available, if you are willing to move it. As you envision where you will place new stones, think of your boulders as the tip of the iceberg emerging from below, and look for spots to place stones as if they had naturally broken away from the larger outcropping and planted themselves in loose soil.

It may be just as practical to remove soil that has accumulated on or around boulders to increase the amount of stone that is visible. For example, if a prominent boulder has a flat upper surface, you might gently clear away any soil from its top and use the soil to begin constructing a level earthen platform behind the boulder. Then add a subtle, low retaining wall to hold the soil in place, and you have a new place for garden plants that will soften the massive presence of the boulder.

Probing for Planting Pockets

Crevices between boulders may be narrow yet deep, which is more than sufficient for many rock-garden plants that spread, such as mosses, rock jasmine (*Androsace lanuginosa*), sea thrift (*Armeria maritima*), and prostrate broom (*Genista pilosa*). Even azaleas can be at home in such an environment. You can investigate the depth of planting pockets with a sturdy knife. You need not remove existing soil before planting. Instead, use a rebar stake to riddle the pocket with holes, and then pack in a gritty soil mix before adding plants.

Where the soil exists in shallow sheets, you can look to low-growing spreading plants to provide vegetative cover. Plants that willingly grow atop stone, such as sedums and sempervivums, often are able to thrive with only 2 inches of soil at their feet if they are allowed to wander freely. In shady settings, numerous native plants, including violets, trilliums, and creeping rues, will eagerly form colonies, provided the soil is prevented from washing away during their period of initial establishment. ■

Gardening among the Ruins

When an old wall or chimney crumbles, part of it remains upright while the majority of it becomes so much rubble on the ground. If you are so fortunate as to have stone ruins on your property, a little work and artistic vision can transform a mess into a beautiful garden structured in stone.

Whether your ruins were once a wall, house, chimney, or springhouse, or even a stone-lined cellar, focus from the outset on the theme that's already before you, which is a place that has been shaped by time. Certainly, you will begin by pulling on a pair of heavy gloves and cleaning up the area, which may hold glass shards, rusted tin cans, and other remnants of human habitation. Also watch out for snakes, poisonous spiders, and threatening plants such as poison ivy or stinging nettle. These natural hazards are easily avoided by undertaking this project in cold weather, but it's still important to put safety first.

As you work, look carefully for stone or concrete footers buried in the ground; many old structures made of wood literally sat upon stone foundations, which can be reused as foundations for rebuilt sections of wall. Set aside weathered stones you find buried in weeds, because ruins usually will need some restoration work to make them safe and attractive.

Pay attention as well to the types of plants that have colonized the area. Although many of them will be too weedy to keep as garden subjects, you can use them as nature's blueprint for what might grow effortlessly in the same niche. For example, you might replace wild brambles with a climbing rose, or plant Boston ivy *(Parthenocissus tricuspidata)* in place of poison ivy or greenbrier. Many old homesites include sturdy old daffodils and other hardy bulbs, which can be left in place or dug and rearranged to restore the outline of the original structure.

Preserving a Legacy

In most cases, you will want to at least partially rebuild the structure that has tumbled down, while leaving some sections in a state of organized disrepair. In order to retain the lines and rhythm of the original stonework, it's helpful to take a few photographs before you begin rearranging stones. You may spend several weeks rebuilding, and it's easy to let your own style take over rather than follow the subtle patterns set out by the stonemason who built the structure in the first place. Should you notice a radical difference

The ruins of a stone house form the framework for a rock garden that meanders outward, with the beds close to the structure neatly restored.

emerging between old and new, a careful study of the photographs will guide you as you position stones.

If possible, preserve at least one corner of a structure that was originally rectangular or square. Besides fostering a sense of enclosure, an interior corner will create a protected planting niche while defining the ruin.

Manage the edges of stone ruins so that they look natural, which usually means having a number of stones tumble into a semi-organized heap. If you have active children, arrange stones so that they don't invite climbing. Most old ruins are so delicate that they can be toppled by climbing kids, who may be seriously injured as a result.

Replacing Old Mortar

If the ruin you are working with was originally held together with mortar, you will likely find a number of weak places where the mortar has broken away. These are simple to repair using ready-mix mortar, which is available at home supply stores. Begin by cleaning out the crevice, using a brush to remove crumbled mortar and sand. Spray the crevice with water, and then carefully pack in mortar that has been thoroughly mixed with water. If you wear heavy rubber gloves, you can use your fingers and a small mason's trowel to push the mortar into the crack. Immediately wipe up any spilled mortar, which will stain weathered stone. Lightly spray all repaired spots with water two or three times a day for three days to help the new mortar cure slowly.

Repaired mortar looks less obvious if it is recessed into the crevices, or you can hide repairs by covering them with plants. Without plants, however, you may need to remortar all of the crevices to avoid a patchwork appearance. ▪

Create the effect of a spring woodland in a container (LEFT) with heuchera, violets, foamflower, columbine, and ferns clustered around a decorative stone.

Blue Atlas cedar (BOTTOM RIGHT) pairs with delicate ferns and foxglove beside a stone-edged woodland pool.

Woodland Ravine

If you live in the mountains of the East or the Northwest, the most natural of all rock gardens is a dreamy woodland scene presided over by majestic trees and carpeted at least in part by lush green mosses. There is a distinct seasonal rhythm to such spots. Sunshine that filters through bare branches in winter and early spring supports the proliferation of spring-blooming native wildflowers, many of which grow in a thin cover of soil over stone. Then, when the trees leaf out, conditions change radically to either moist or dry shade. Summer becomes the season of ferns and vines, perhaps punctuated by a few small shrubs. As leaves flutter down in the fall, the garden is clothed in brown and gold until it is flushed clean by winter rains or snows. Bare stones feature a tapestry of lichens and mosses through the winter, and the cycle begins again at the first hint of spring.

A healthy dose of gentle artistry is involved in keeping this type of rock garden, but one must always be mindful of plans and patterns that nature decides to etch into the site. The movement of water must be considered, too, along with the scouring effect of floodwaters that flow for a few hours after heavy rainstorms and then disappear for days, weeks, and sometimes months at a time.

We gardeners are often quick to decide where we want plants, moss, or stone, and then we're surprised when nature changes the balance. Yet this type of rock garden can be endlessly fascinating if you view it as a contrast between stone and not-stone, which may be plants, mosses, lichens, or even mud. The guideline used in classical alpine rock gardening, which is to have about one-third of the area visible as stone, applies to the woodland rock garden as well.

Spring Ephemerals

Collectively known as spring ephemerals, many of the trilliums, toad lilies, dwarf iris, and woodland rues have evolved to grow on rock, and they wisely become dormant in summer. Native-plant nurseries are a treasure trove of these woodland wonders, which range from well-known blue phlox *(Phlox divaricata)* and goosefoot geranium *(Geranium maculatum)* to less common bloodroot *(Sanguinaria canadensis)* and Dutchman's breeches *(Dicentra cucullaria)*. Late winter is the best time to set out these and similar native plants, which often grow from shallow rhizomes (thick, knobby sections of root). As little as 2 to 3 inches of soil over rock is sufficient for their needs.

Fantastic Ferns

Despite their delicate appearance, ferns become iron-clad members of a shady plant community once they are established. With the exception of Christmas fern (*Polystichum acrostichoides*), few ferns are evergreen in climates where the soil freezes hard in winter. Yet excellent deciduous ferns exist for every climate, and it is always best to go with species that grow wild in your area. Beware of extremely large ferns, such as cinnamon fern and royal fern (*Osmunda* species), which can overwhelm a rock garden with their sheer size. Most ferns benefit from a rather deep planting pocket well amended with organic matter, and they are particularly fond of leaf mold.

Miracle Mosses

A wooded rock garden cries out for mosses, which often appear spontaneously if the site is sufficiently moist. If handled carefully, stones that are already nicely colonized by mosses when they are brought to the garden will retain their green cover, but you should never expect smooth, newly cut stone to serve well as a home for moss. Despite what you think you see, moss does not actually grow on stone. Rather, it grows in organic matter that accumulates in small crevices, often following lichens in slow natural succession. So smooth stone just won't do for moss — it needs those crevices in order to get established.

Growing moss in crevices or on the ground around stones is quite easy and is usually a simple matter of importing hand-sized pieces from areas close to your home, pressing it into place, and then keeping it damp for several weeks. Moss likes lean, acidic soil conditions (with a pH around 5.5), so the soil mix for moss is a simple half-and-half mixture of peat moss and sand. Try several types, because conditions that are pleasing to one moss may be distasteful to another. Maintaining moss consists of blowing or raking off debris in early winter and pulling out weeds first thing in spring.

Plants for Rock Gardens

When reading books or nursery catalogs, pay close attention when the word "saxatile" is used to describe a plant. *Saxum* is Latin for rock, so a plant with saxatile inclinations is likely to grow well in close company with stone.

As previously mentioned, many of the best rock garden plants are naturally petite, with fine textures that marry beautifully with the smooth finish of stone. But don't let the small size of blooming rock garden plants fool you. Part of the magic of rock garden plants is that their blossoms appear extra large and vibrant compared with the plants that produced them.

In addition to the plants listed here, those suggested for steps on pages 96 to 99 and for walls on pages 128 to 131 would also make excellent additions to rock gardens, provided they work well with the scale of the stone used, as well as fit in well with neighboring plants.

Stonecress *(Aethionema grandiflorum)*

Also known as Persian candytuft, stonecress is a small, shrubby sprawler with attractive blue-gray foliage that is nearly hidden by the numerous pale to deep pink blooms that appear in late spring. Ideal for rock gardens, screes, or the top of a stone wall, stonecress requires slightly alkaline soil. Hardiness ranges from Zones 6 to 8. Stonecress is often evergreen where winters are mild. Individual plants are not always long-lived, so it's wise to root a few stem cuttings each summer so you always have young, vigorous replacements.

Rock Cress *(Arabis* species)

Most rock cresses are true alpines, so they demand the fresh air and fast drainage of rock gardens. Willing spreaders, they do a fine job of cascading over boulders or walls. Hardiness varies with species, but gardeners in Zones 4 and 8 should have no trouble finding sufficiently cold-hardy cresses. The *Arabis caucasia* 'Variegata' shown here has white flowers and white- or pink-edged leaves. All rock cresses bloom in spring, and benefit from shearing back by half their size in early summer.

Sea Thrift (*Armeria maritima*)

Truly a dry soil plant, this compact little perennial grows wild on Scotland's rocky cliffs. As long as sea thrift gets plenty of sun and neutral, sandy soil with excellent drainage, it is easily grown in Zones 3 to 9. Plants grow 6 to 8 inches tall and form foot-wide clumps, which can be dug and divided in fall. Spring flowers are in various shades of pink and sometimes white. Never fertilize sea thrift with anything stronger than a little compost, and water sparingly, if at all. The cultivar shown here is 'Ornament'.

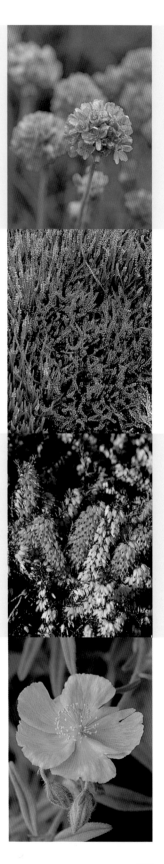

Heather (*Calluna vulgaris*)

Often called Scotch heather or ling, named cultivars include numerous small, spreading plants that are just the right size for sunny rock gardens. Old favorites for rock gardens include those shown here: 'Tib' with deep pink flowers (center), 'Silver Knight' (left), and 'White Knight' (right). All need lean, acidic soil and usually bloom in late summer and fall, when few other plants offer color. Heathers are best adapted in Zones 5 to 7, but warm exposures in Zone 3 are often acceptable.

Spring Heath (*Erica carnea*)

Sometimes called alpine heather, spring heath is an 8- to 10-inch-tall evergreen that forms thick mats of foliage topped by pink or white flowers in late winter. A slow grower best adapted in Zones 5 to 7, it needs moist, acidic soil with excellent drainage. It thrives on plenty of organic matter in the soil, such as peat moss, but can be killed by fertilizer. For best appearance, shear back the bloom-bearing stems after the flowers fade. The cultivar shown here is 'King George'.

Helianthemum (*Helianthemum nummularium*)

Commonly called sunrose or rockrose, this drought-tolerant species typically produces bright yellow, red, or bicolored flowers in early summer, though some cultivars, such as the 'Wisley Pink' shown here, bloom pink or white. Plants grow to 12 inches high and spread into 18-inch-wide mats. 'Wisley Pink' grows in Zones 6 to 8. Many selections will rebloom in the fall if sheared back in midsummer. As their name suggests, full sun is the most essential requirement for helianthemum.

Lewisia (*Lewisia* species)

The most famous lewisia is Montana's state flower, the bitterroot *(L. rediviva)*. While beautiful, it is but one *Lewisia* species to grow in a dry-climate rock garden. Arid areas of Zones 6 to 8 are also ideal for cliff maids (*L.* Cotyledon Hybrids), one of which is shown here. These grow 12 inches tall. After flowering in spring, the plants of all lewisias become dormant through summer. Dry summers are required, because the plants quickly rot when exposed to summer rain.

Narcissus (*Narcissus* species)

Large-flowered trumpets and other daffodils make a great show in the spring land-scape, but look for daintier cultivars for the rock garden. Tremendously hardy and dependable, *N.* 'Suzy' (shown here) and cultivars of *N. cyclamineus* such as 'Jack Snipe' are ideal, as are miniatures such as 'Tête-a-Tête'. Set out bulbs in the fall and allow the foliage to remain intact after the flowers fade in spring. It will die back naturally in early summer.

Primrose (*Primula* species)

Primula species number in the hundreds, with huge variation in size, hardiness, and blooming habit. A few species, such as *P. auricula,* are hardy to Zone 3; *P. sieboldii* (shown here) grows in Zones 3 to 8. Local rock gardeners can steer you toward tried-and-true favorites, which are always a good place to start. Most primroses need rich, moist soil, so they are best planted near the base of a rock garden or in partial shade, but some alpine species need dry conditions, especially in winter.

Saxifrage (*Saxifraga* species)

All cultivars of this huge tribe of plants grow beautifully in rock nooks and crannies. Leaf shape and color vary with species, and many feature delicate silver beading along leaf edges. Most rock-garden selections bloom white or pink in early summer, and leaves become reddish bronze as the weather cools in the fall. Generally adapted in Zones 4 to 9, saxifrages appreciate partial shade in warm climates. The *S. cotyledon* shown here grows in Zones 4 to 6.

Stonecrop *(Sedum kamtschaticum)*

The same hardy little succulents used to plant a stone wall or carpet a stone path make fine additions to the rock garden, where they can be counted upon to thrive in the driest pockets. Shown here is 'Rosy Glow', a clump-forming perennial that features cherry red flowers from late summer to fall on 12-inch-tall stems. Other cultivars in this species that is adapted to Zones 4 to 9 are 'Variegatum' and 'Wiehenstephaner Gold'.

Sempervivum *(Sempervivum* species)

Long known as houseleeks or hen-and-chicks, these beautiful succulents sometimes have trouble with cold winter weather but are generally hardy to Zone 6. They are easily lifted in the fall, and they can be kept in a cool garage through winter. Sempervivums are often shared among gardeners, because starting a new planting is a simple matter of breaking off a stem and planting it in any soil. Sempervivums seldom bloom, but their bold texture is sufficient to earn them a place in the rock garden.

Cactus (numerous species)

With few exceptions, cacti are not hardy where winters are severe, so their use in rock gardens is largely limited to the Southwest. The showiest species produce bright flowers in summer, especially if given supplemental water and fertilizer in the spring. Some excellent species include peanut cactus *(Echinops chamaecereus),* extremely hardy "little" cactus *(Escobaria vivipara),* chin cactus *(Gymnocalycium* spp.), dozens of species of globe-shaped *Mammillaria,* and *Notocactus haselbergii* (shown here).

CHAPTER 6

STONE, WATER & GARDENS

In a garden setting, stone and water interact in ways that delight the senses. Water mirrors the reflection of a wall or stone backdrop along with the plants that grow along the water's edge. And if

some of the water in the pond moves via a fall or fountain, stone can be used to alter its course and enhance its sound. Best of all, the appearance of water and wet rocks magically makes us feel cooler. On hot days, it's hard to resist the impulse to get close enough to dip your hand into the water, and then linger as you watch ripples move gently across the water's surface.

A formal stone fountain looks perfectly at home in a circle of cut stone framed with boxwood and low-growing perennials.

Designing with Water and Stone

There are probably lovely water gardens that do not include stone, but I've never seen one. Stone appears in most man-made water gardens, because at least some edges of a pond, stream, or waterfall must be held firm with heavy stone. Yet the marriage of water and stone is primal as well, because wherever we see water in nature, we almost always see stone.

A water feature also opens up endless possibilities for gardening with plants that grow in water. True aquatic plants such as water lilies and lotus can be grown in submerged pots; parrot's feather and other floating and minimally rooted plants flourish in the corners of ponds; and you can use plants that prefer shallow water or boggy conditions to fill the space along the water's edge. Indeed, water gardens need plants, which serve as biological filters to keep the water clean. Finally, a few fish add to a water garden's allure and keep it free of mosquitoes and other unwanted insects.

You will likely enjoy a water garden so much that you will want to have it in a place visible from many parts of your landscape, especially areas where you like to sit and relax. If you intend to grow water lilies or other blooming plants, the site should get at least four hours of direct sunlight, or six hours in a cool climate. All edges of the pool itself must be level. To achieve level edges, you can modify the site somewhat as you dig the pond, but serious slopes are unsuitable for a large pond. Instead, create a waterfall or stream on a slope, with a small, deep pond at the base to serve as a reservoir for the circulating water.

The depth of the pond is dependent on your climate, the way water moves through the pond, and the plants you hope to grow there. A depth of 16 to 18 inches is fine for most plants, though it is always a good idea to have a deeper pocket under a place where water enters the pond forcefully.

Shallow ledges along the pond's edge are invaluable for hosting "marginal" plants — those that grow in shallow water along the water's edge. Ledges increase the diversity of plants you can grow, and they soften the edges of the pond so they look more natural.

Keep in mind that many aquatic plants react poorly to constant turbulence. There is an inherent conflict between water lilies and waterfalls. If running water is the only design your site can accommodate, garden along the edges of your water feature rather than in it. A broad, still pond, on the other hand, is ideal for showcasing stately lotus or long-lived hardy water lilies.

When water is pushed up and over a broad stone that works as a shallow sill (LEFT), its fall becomes more musical and dramatic.

Pendulous ornamental grasses growing above a stone retaining wall (RIGHT) mirror the cascading water in the dramatic falls below.

Friendly Fish

Although any life form that inhabits nearby streams and lakes stands a good chance of surviving in a water garden, two types of fish — goldfish and koi — are the favorites of water gardeners. Plain old goldfish, called comets, purchased from any pet store are surprisingly tough and hardy and can be left in the garden year-round in Zone 5 and warmer areas.

I realize that saying anything negative about koi may offend some people as much as criticizing Labrador retrievers would. However, koi are large, active fish, so they need a large pond. But their main drawback is that they eat aquatic plants, and this can severely limit how much water gardening you are able to do.

The meeting ground between the two extremes is butterfly koi, a cross between comet goldfish and koi carp. Butterfly koi often have showy fins, like fancy goldfish, but they don't grow to be nearly as large as more robust hybrid koi.

Regardless of species, the safest stocking rate for your pond is 1 inch of fish per square foot of pond surface area (length times width). Fish inches are measured nose to tailfin tip, and it's wise to base your estimate on the mature size of your fish. Most goldfish top out at 4 to 6 inches in length, while koi can grow to be a foot long. If you have too many fish, you will have to feed them regularly, and you'll need to include a filter in your system.

A placid pond in a woodland setting (LEFT) is an ideal place for small fish; frogs and turtles may move in as well.

Weathered boulders interspersed with submerged and floating plants (RIGHT) create a completely natural effect.

Soft Transitions

The greatest challenge in designing a water garden is to make it appear to belong in the landscape. Particularly in level sites, it's far too easy to install a water feature, ring it with a necklace of stone, and then wonder why it sticks out like a sore thumb. To keep this from happening, you will need to use your imagination to orchestrate ways to integrate water, stone, and plants into the site your landscape has to offer.

It is a grave mistake to assume that all edges of a water feature must be trimmed in stone. If you want a natural effect, it is much wiser to do what nature does, which is to clothe at least some edges of the water with lush plants. Use plants that grow in shallow water, for instance, and plant them in a submerged shelf a few inches below the surface, or grow them in the soil surrounding the pond, so that they seem almost to softly creep toward it or cascade to tickle the water's edge.

Alternatively, you can design a very formal water feature that does not presume to mimic nature. For example, a circular reflecting pool is obviously man-made, so it will look best with highly refined stonework and gracefully symmetrical plantings. To capture plant reflections effectively, study the sun's path over the area before positioning plants. For this approach, you need a feeling of clean simplicity, which probably means using cut stone rather than more primitive stacking stone.

Filters and Pumps

A small pocket pond that includes the right balance of plants and fish can be so ecologically stable that it requires no additional filter. Twice I have built and enjoyed such natural water gardens, which need to include enough plants to cover a little more than half of the surface area of the water, and absolutely no more than 2 inches of fish per square foot of surface area. Such a pond becomes a beautiful little wet world in which plants clean and oxygenate the water, while fish keep it free of mosquitoes.

In larger water features that include numerous fish, there are several good reasons to filter water. Simply put, fish food and excrement make water so rich that it tends to host large amounts of algae, which make the water turn cloudy and green. If uncontrolled, bacteria and chemicals accumulate, which results in a murky pond and sick fish.

Pond suppliers sell boxes, called biomechanical filters, that address this problem two ways. They run mechanically, on water pushed through them by a pump, and clean the water biologically by subjecting it to processing by bacteria that live within the filter. Biomechanical filters may be filled with a number of materials, such as lava rock, foam, special fiber mats, or any small objects that host beneficial bacteria while allowing water to percolate through them (plastic hair curlers are said to be wonderful). However, percolation must be *slow,* or the biological processes involved won't work.

Rock Filters

It's not always necessary to purchase a biomechanical filter. When working with stone on a sloping site, see if there is some way you can create a small reservoir above the main area of your water feature that can be filled with 12 inches or so of rough gravel or lava rock, with an outlet at the bottom through which the filtered water can run into the pond below. In other words, a pipe attached to a small pump in your main pond delivers water to the reservoir-filter and then carries it through the gravel into the main pond via an outlet pipe hidden between stones. When you notice a serious reduction in flow, you'll know it's time to clean out the reservoir; you'll probably need to do this once or twice a year. Do keep in mind that this is a biological system, so it's okay for the rocks in the filter to be slimy. Leaves, dirt, and other debris that block the trickle of water are the real reasons you'll need to clean a natural rock filter.

Water flows from a pump in this container water garden through plastic piping hidden within the stone wall and then spills over a stone back into the container.

A single large-capacity pump in the reservoir at the bottom of these falls keeps water moving along its course.

Running a Pump

Any type of fountain, bubbler, or waterfall requires the use of a pump. Although solar-powered pumps are now available from garden and pond supply stores, they move relatively small amounts of water (usually enough for only a small fountain). Electrically powered pumps vary in size and are rated according to how much water they pump in gallons per hour (GPH). You can run a small fountain with a pump that moves only about 200 GPH, but pumps that are powerful enough to push water up and over a waterfall range from 325 GPH to more than 3,000 GPH. Your choice will depend on how much water you want to move and how far up it must be pushed. More information on choosing a pump for a stream or waterfall is given later in this chapter. Also, you can get advice from a local dealer or call customer service at one of the large mail-order pond suppliers.

Incidentally, all pumps include a mesh or foam filter that keeps debris from being pushed through the mechanism, but additional biological filtration (discussed above) is usually necessary in large ponds that contain more than 300 gallons of water. Because the pump and filter must work in tandem, they should be planned and purchased together. This is one situation where local expertise is invaluable.

You will also need an expert electrician to install a special weatherproof outdoor outlet that includes a ground fault circuit breaker. In some areas local ordinances require that a licensed electrician do this job. In addition to running your pump, this outlet can be used to power outdoor lighting as well.

A collar of cut stone mortared in place keeps the edges of this pond level, essential for holding the water in.

Ways to Hold Water

The popularity of water gardening has made it easier than ever to create a water garden of any shape, size, and configuration you desire. Your first decision will be to choose between a rigid form and a fish-safe flexible liner. Most home supply stores sell prefabricated, rigid plastic forms, which are set into holes sculpted into the ground, as well as flexible rubber liners, which mold themselves to the shape of the excavated site. Small tub-shaped containers also are available, along with broad bowls roomy enough to accommodate a plant or two along with a token comet goldfish.

Preformed, rigid pond liners are fine for small water features, and many manufacturers provide pamphlets that show how you can link different forms together to create curves and small falls. Rigid liners do have some drawbacks, including size and installation requirements: They must be set into carefully excavated holes that are perfectly level at both the bottom and the rim. One trick that will make this easier is to first lay 2 inches of sand under the liner; you will then be able to make the necessary small adjustments more easily than you would over solid ground. The sand also helps insulate the liner from small heaves in surrounding ground.

Another good technique is to fill the installed liner with water at the same time that you backfill soil along the sides. As you do so, stop often to check the level of the top edges of the form, which often shift a bit once the form fills with water.

For those who want to contain water in a more natural shape of their own choice, flexible rubber liners are a popular option. Pond suppliers often stock huge rolls of the stuff and cut it to any size you desire. Although they are not cheap, pond liners that are safe for fish are typically 45 mils thick, and they can be expected to last for many years.

The first step in installing a flexible liner is to mark the edges of where your pond will go, which you can do with a garden hose, rope, or can of spray paint. Study your plan for a day or two to make sure you have a good idea of how sun and shade will affect the site.

Also consider where in the pond you will sculpt shelves for marginal plants. A good rule of thumb is to have one-third of the perimeter include 6-inch-wide shelves that will sit about 6 inches below the water when the pond is full. If you locate these shelves along the back of the pond, plants growing there won't block your view of the water. A second, shallower shelf should encircle the entire pond. This is called the rock shelf, and its sole purpose is to provide a place to set rocks to anchor the rubber liner. Those stones will be submerged most of the time but they ensure that the liner will be hidden from view if the water level drops because of drought or the operation of a pump and a waterfall. Finally, additional broad stones should be placed atop the ones on the rock shelf.

Create a water garden in a single afternoon by sinking a pre-formed tub into the ground and trimming the edges with stone.

Bringing a Water Garden to Life

Tap water contains chlorine and other chemicals that are toxic to plants and fish, so plan to let your new pond sit for two weeks before turning it into a garden. You can go ahead and install your pump and filter if they are included in your plan, and it's fine to get plants situated in rock crevices and planting pockets around your new water feature. Don't worry if there's a little dirt in the pond from construction or from nearby planting activities. Water gardens do contain soil, after all, and some plants like a mucky bottom. However, most of the ones you grow will be planted in containers, which are usually set upon bricks or other supports to adjust their depth.

Get most of your plants situated before you introduce fish. And, even though comets are tough little critters, expect a few to go belly up within days after you bring them home. Those that survive the move will probably be with you for years, so you may as well go ahead and give them names. ▪

Installing a Flexible Liner

Digging a pond is slow work, and you will need a place to stockpile your excavated soil. You'll also need to be meticulous in checking the level of the upper edges over and over again.

Excavate the Site with Level Edges

In a very wide pond, you may need to install boards over the excavation site to check the level in every direction. I think it's best to wait until the excavation is nearly complete to buy your liner. When you calculate how much liner to buy, measure the surface area of the pond as well as its depth, and allow extra liner so that it will extend at least 6 inches over the edge of the pond.

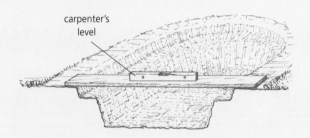

carpenter's level

Install the Liner and Begin Filling the Pond

Unfold and spread out the liner over the excavated site, eliminating as many wrinkles and folds as you can where the liner tends to bunch up. These will flatten out under the weight of the water.

Liners always need to be tucked and folded as the pond is filled, so take off your shoes and get right in there, for this is part of the fun. You'll need to push the liner around to get rid of air pockets, too. Rubber liner stretches slightly under the weight of water, so it's wise to fill the pond only halfway at first. Also, you will actually be in the water as you place many of the stones around the edges, and it's more comfortable to work in shallow water.

Cover the Rock Shelf and Finish Adding Water

Pack stacking stone into the rock shelf, using gravel and shim stones to get a tight fit. Visit a natural pond and observe how the rocks are positioned, so that you can imitate their unplanned appearance. Flat coping stones will go atop the shelf, so fix any wobbles in the rock shelf now. With the shelf stones in place, finish filling the pond with water, and trim away excess liner with a utility knife.

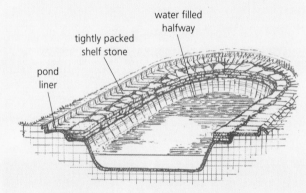

water filled halfway

tightly packed shelf stone

pond liner

Overhang the Edges with Coping Stones

Finally, place coping stones around the edges, trying to have an overhang of about 2 inches. This will both hide the liner from view and keep fish from jumping out of the pond. Where you foresee places for plants near the pond's edge, allow interesting breaks in the stonework, or substitute a small rounded boulder for a flat coping stone.

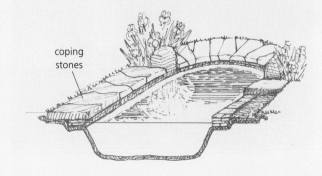

coping stones

Fine Points of Digging

Before installing the liner, it is a good idea to spread 2 inches of damp sand over the excavated site. This will make the bottom of the pond softer and will minimize gaps between the liner and its base. It's hard to get sand to stay packed against nearly perpendicular edges, so you might line the sides with strips of old carpeting. When I created a little pond that I knew would become a favorite swimming hole for some overheated dogs, I laid a piece of old carpeting beneath the liner as an extra cushion against holes from dog claws. If you don't have to worry about dogs or deer getting into your pond or if it's unlikely that sharp rocks or roots might work their way through the soil and puncture the liner, you can lay the liner directly on excavated ground.

Equipped with a flexible liner and surrounded by plants and stone, a pond can present a natural appearance in almost any shape you desire. Here, some ornaments and colorful fish create even more visual interest in this sunbathed pool.

Pocket Pond

The best proof that truly wonderful things come in small packages can be found in a pocket pond — a small pool dug into the ground, made watertight with a liner, and landscaped with stone. Although limited in size, a pocket pond brings the wonder of water to the landscape and provides a place to grow aquatic plants. And because it is situated at ground level, a pocket pond naturally attracts wildlife, including birds, butterflies, frogs, and occasionally thirsty raccoons.

When well sited, a pocket pond will resemble a quiet spring. It can be as small as a 3-foot-wide circle dug 18 inches into the ground, which will hold about 100 gallons of water. This is roomy enough for several aquatic plants, a trio of goldfish, and accompanying stones that match the pond in scale. And, unless you want a small fountain or bubbler, a pond of this size has no need for pumps or filters.

Because it's small, a pocket pond is an excellent project for beginners, and it's an ideal way to incorporate stone into your landscape. To make the most of the reflective potential of such a pond, plan from the beginning to have a vertical stone structure or a piece of statuary flanked by upright plants at either the back or one side of your pocket pond. Then feature the pond at night with uplighting. Small lights installed at ground level will set objects around the water aglow and, in turn, these focal points will be reflected on the water's surface.

Anticipate Expansion

Unless your yard is truly tiny, anticipate that sooner or later your pocket pond will probably evolve into something larger, such as a reservoir pool for a little waterfall (see page 184). Or someday you might spread out sideways, adding a shallow bog garden to a side of the pond that is prone to flooding. Once you have lived with a pocket pond for a while, you will begin to see new possibilities to expand the ways you use water in your landscape, especially in the company of stone. ■

A small hidden pump at the bottom of a pocket pond (LEFT) pushes a trickle of water upward.

Even a small pond (RIGHT) can be designed to provide a secluded shelter among the rocks for fish.

Focus on Shape

A pocket pond becomes an instant focal point in the landscape, but that does not mean it must go in the middle of your outdoor space. In small yards, many gardeners tuck a pocket pond into a corner and let the rest of the landscape flow in its direction. A pond that is circular or oval in shape naturally offsets the straight lines of a corner, and circles also have a strong unifying effect that naturally ties the landscape together.

Be sure to include a walkway or a broad landing to make it easy to get close to the water, and use the same kind of stone in the walkway that you use to secure the edges of the pond. Put plants to work for you, too. One simple approach is to let crevice plants such as ajuga, pearlwort, or sedums scramble down the walkway and up to the pond's edge. These plantings will knit the scene together, creating a natural effect that makes the garden appear to have evolved on its own.

A small, placid pool trimmed in smooth stones works as a refreshing oasis within a garden lush with flowering shrubs and perennials.

Digging In

You can use either a preformed rigid liner or a rubber liner to build a pocket pond. Follow the basic steps for pond building outlined on pages 168 to 171. When doing any extensive excavation work in an established landscape, it's smart to collect several large pieces of scrap plywood and use them to cover spots of lawn or other plants that you want to protect from construction violence.

If your plans call for a stone wall behind the pond, you can work on both projects simultaneously, using the soil excavated from the pond site to fill in behind the wall. Complete the wall first, or you will be dropping sharp rocks, mud, and other debris into the new pond. Do allow at least 8 inches between the edge of the pond and the wall's foundation so you will have a level edge for coping stones or a spot for growing cascading plants, or perhaps both.

Quiet Water, Quiet Plants

A pocket pond is a peaceful presence in the landscape, so I think it's best to emphasize aquatic plants that have a serene demeanor, both inside and outside the pond. Water lily leaves float gracefully on the water's surface, and their flat roundness contrasts beautifully with clumps of upright dwarf cattail or water iris installed just inside the water's edge. Or you might use your pond to host dwarf lotus, which can be easily confined to tubs placed within the pond.

You should play it cool with the flowers you grow around your pocket pond, too. Stick with perennials that bloom in soft shades of pink, blue, and white, and add soft-textured annuals wherever you can fit them for extra summer color. In most cases, you will find that plants that produce small flowers make the best companions for a pocket pond, because they defer happily to water, which is always the enchanting star of the show.

Walking on Water

A series of stones that leads you to walk across water is rich with metaphors. The ritual of crossing from one place to another and of being within the water and outside it at the same time is powerful. As your feet meet the firmness of the intermittent bridge over water, you are fleetingly held in limbo between wet and dry, liquid and solid. Or, if you are a child, you are simply delighted by the challenge of crossing water without getting wet.

If these images and symbols are irresistible to you, perhaps you'd rather walk on water than simply look at it. A walkable stretch of water does differ from the types of water gardens one usually thinks of, and it's wise to design a water feature intended for crossing with this purpose in mind. However, it's certainly possible to incorporate stone stepping-stones into a placid pool or a running stream (described on pages 179 and 180) if you so desire.

Companion Stones

Bear in mind that the more challenging the crossing appears, the more important it is to have solid threshold stones on either side that emphasize the fact that one is, indeed, *invited* to cross the water. This will be clear if you have a walkway that leads directly to the crossing. Remember, too, that stepping-stones placed in water will appear more natural if other stones nearby protrude above the water's surface. These can be rounded or angular in shape, because their purpose is to provide congenial company for the stones that make up the crossing. ■

Creative Crossings

One characteristic that successful stepping-stone crossings share is that the water they cross is quite shallow. Rather than the 18- to 24-inch depth typical of most water gardens, the section to be traversed should usually be only 4 to 8 inches deep. The reasons for this are both practical and aesthetic. The stepping-stones should rise only 1 to 2 inches above the water's surface, and it is far easier to locate and install stones with flat tops and bottoms less than 10 inches thick than to do the same with massive slabs. Crossing shallow water also feels safer than tiptoeing across water that is so deep that you can't see the bottom.

You can alter the level of excitement in the crossing through your choice and placement of stepping-stones. Large stones placed close together in a straight line offer passage that is safe and sure, but not very thrilling. When stepping-stones are placed farther apart, in a curving or zigzag pattern, the crossing becomes slower and more mysterious. Another option is to use stones of varying sizes, with one or two large slabs linked to the shore by smaller, irregular stepping-stones.

Landscape gardening also plays a role in creative crossings, and here you have yet another unique opportunity to use stones that work so well with nearby plants that each seems to depend on the other. Tall plants near the crossing create a reassuring feeling of enclosure, as when water iris or cattails are so close you can almost reach out and touch them. Or you can create a feeling of serenity by framing the crossing with soft, mounding evergreen shrubs planted just outside the water's edge.

One way to look at plants you might place near a crossing is to imagine the answer they might give to the question "What if I fall?" Naturally, roses and other prickly plants are too threatening to consider, while soft ferns, grasses, or dwarf Japanese maples would be much more reassuring.

Steadying Steps

When installing stepping-stones in the ground, you always have the option of molding the hole to irregularities in the stones' surfaces. In most cases, you can't do this in a water garden, and you may have trouble getting stones to stay put when they are placed on a slick rubber liner. Small shim stones may have sharp edges that will puncture the liner, so they can't be used to steady wobbly stepping-stones unless you use a protective pad, such as a scrap piece of carpeting, beneath the main stone and the shims you use to hold it firmly in place.

There are other options. One is to use cement to fix stepping-stones in place, but this must be done when the pond is dry. And whenever cement is used within a water garden, you should take the additional step of sealing it to slow the leaching of lime and other chemicals into the water.

If you'd rather skip cement, you might consider having your stepping-stones sit in a 2-inch-deep layer of mud. As long as the water is reasonably still, rounded river rocks placed over the mud will hide it from view. Wandering roots from nearby aquatic plants will also help keep the mud from shifting to where it is not wanted.

A series of stepping-stones across a shallow pond allows visitors to traverse the water with confidence and get closer to both plants and fish.

Running Water

Creating a stream garden is a little more complicated than building a placid pool, but a stream provides a number of rewards that make the extra effort worthwhile. The music of moving water is intoxicating, as is the reassuring flow of sparkling water. In order to keep the water flowing, you will need to have a location where there is a change in elevation; but because stream gardens are narrow, they often can fit into tight spaces too small for a pond. If you have a large space, you can design a stream that follows an S curve, filling the area. You might instead add interest by including a sharp turn or two between the beginning and the end of the run.

The mechanics of creating an artificial stream are pretty straightforward. You will need a pool or reservoir at the lowest level, equipped with a pump that pushes water up through a pipe to the top of the stream. The pool can be a water garden or a buried reservoir, hidden from view by shrubs. Make sure that you leave the pump in a spot that is easily accessible when the pump needs cleaning.

A stream garden is a closed system, so getting the right combination of pump, reservoir, and stream is crucial. A stream that is very long or wide requires a larger pump and reservoir than a small one, because when the pump is running, it will remove substantial amounts of water from the reservoir or pond. If the pond is too small, it will flood badly when the pump is turned off and will appear parched when the pump is running.

A stream need not be wide or even carry a great volume of water to be effective. Here, a quiet narrow stream lavishly edged with low-growing plants is peaceful and soothing.

Estimating Operating Volume

The amount of water that runs through a course of water is called the operating volume. To create a system that can handle the volume, you can calculate how much water will flow through your stream and compare it with how much water is available in the pond or reservoir. Don't worry if math isn't your strongest suit: The table below shows what proportions of pond size to stream length are required to maintain the correct level of water in the pond when the pump is running. The estimates are based on a streambed 3 feet wide filled with 3 inches of water. Be sure to include the length of vertical drops when measuring length. Pond depth doesn't matter, because your primary concern is what goes on at the surface. Generally, a drop in water level of 2 inches or less is tolerable provided the marginal area is attractively dressed with plants and stone. If the pond is too small, or the stream too large, the water level will drop too much when the pump is turned on and the reservoir will flood when it is turned off. ∎

Proper Proportions of Pond Size to Stream Length

Size of Pond	Length of Stream	Drop in Water
5' x 5'	8'	2"
6' x 6'	10'	1.74"
8' x 8'	10'	.98"
8' x 8'	15'	1.46"
10' x 10'	15'	.94"
10' x 10'	20'	1.25"
10' x 12'	20'	1.04"
10' x 12'	25'	1.3"

The Fine Points

As you design a streambed or waterfall, never lose sight of the importance of retaining water. The pipe that carries water from the pond to the top of the stream is usually buried outside the streambed, and it's important to bury it where it can be dug up should it develop leaks. Gophers, for example, have been known to chew through plastic pipe; equally damaging are tree roots, which sometimes enter pipes through small cracks, causing them to fail.

You will also need to lay a rubber liner on the streambed, which should be excavated and prepared in the same way as is done for a pond (see page 170). If your stream meanders, you will probably use pieces of liner rather than one continuous sheet. Overlap seams by at least 2 inches, with the top piece of liner overlapping in the direction of the water flow. Arrange folds this way, too, so that they fold downward with the slope. If you work from the bottom of the elevation upward, these factors will take care of themselves.

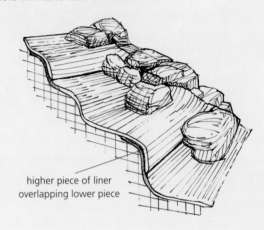

higher piece of liner
overlapping lower piece

Arranging Stones

Because water flows both above and beneath stones that line a streambed, some people mortar stones in place to keep more of the water at the surface. Home supply stores also sell spray poly foam that can be used for this purpose. However, I think it is best not to fix stones in place from the outset, because until your stream is operational, you don't know exactly how the stones and the water will interact. Later, if you're not satisfied with the stability of your stones, you can always turn off the pump, let the streambed dry out, and move in with mortar or poly foam.

Besides, much of the fun of having a stream is enjoying its music, which can easily be altered by moving stones from place to place. You can experiment endlessly with the sounds of your water by wedging stones in different ways, having water fall onto smooth stones, or creating narrows in the stream to make the water rush through with more force.

A stone mortared on the edge of a larger boulder (ABOVE) can intensify the rush of water that is diverted to each side of it.

A relatively small pond (RIGHT) is refreshed by a lively flowing stream. Plants with spiky or fine foliage contrast nicely with the smooth stones.

Constructing a Waterfall

You can build a waterfall in which the water rushes down in a single cascade, but most people like the effect achieved by having water fall in tiers, or steps. Constructing such a waterfall combines the techniques used to build steps (see pages 86 and 87) with those used to construct a stream (pages 179 to 181).

Waterfalls typically include a small reservoir at the top and a larger, deeper one at the bottom. The top reservoir is optional, for you can have water flow directly from a hidden pipe. The fall area usually requires both a continuous (or lapped) liner that underlies the entire water run and smaller pieces of liner installed to channel water over spillway stones.

Before arranging stones within the waterfall itself, excavate both ponds and the waterfall site and install the base liner. Go ahead and place large stones that will hold the liner in place along the top and edges, and then turn on the water. This will help settle the folds of the liner, and it will tell you much about exactly how the water wants to flow.

How you place stone within the waterfall determines flow patterns and how the water sounds as it falls, so just resolve to get wet and turn the water on and off frequently as you settle stones in place. Work from the bottom up, using smaller pieces of liner to channel water slightly upward over the lip of each fall. As you work, you will discover places along the edge of the waterfall where water is not inclined to flow. In these areas, trim the liner as needed, and then arrange stones to form planting frames for plants.

Flat stones that form a shelf at the edge of waterfall steps create dramatic effects, which is especially nice in small waterfalls that don't push much water. Set spillway stones as level as possible to increase the width of the sill. Don't worry if you can see a bit of the top liner at the back of spillway stones. Algae and tumbled bits of gravel will soon make it disappear.

Two factors give this waterfall (FACING PAGE) a high-energy feeling: a narrow water run to increase water depth, and large differences in elevation.

Water flows gently and musically from a series of large stone slabs (ABOVE), where water-loving ferns and sedums clothe the rock faces.

Plants for Water Gardens

Plants that must have wet feet are divided into three large categories: submerged plants that grow in pots beneath 4 to 12 inches of water, floating plants that drag their roots with them as they float from place to place, and marginal or shallow-water plants that thrive in wet or flooded soil.

Water gardeners also differentiate between hardy plants, which usually can be left in the water garden year-round, and tropicals, which must be either sacrificed at the end of the season or brought indoors and kept through the winter in tubs. Tropical water lilies and lotus are worth the trouble of maintaining them through the seasons, but with more common tropicals, such as water lettuce, it's fine to treat them as annuals and get new plants each spring.

Don't assume that all plants for your water garden must be bought. If you have access to a stream or lake on private property, ask the owner's permission to pluck out a few natives to try in your water garden. You may be surprisingly pleased with the results.

Marsh Marigold *(Caltha palustris)*

A marginal plant to grow in wet soil along the pond's edge, marsh marigold emerges in spring, produces waxy yellow blooms for several weeks, and then dies back in early summer. Easily grown in Zones 3 to 7, marsh marigold prefers acid soil. Full sun will make the plant grow upright, while shade promotes a more sprawling growth habit. The popular cultivar shown here is 'Flore Pleno', with double yellow flowers.

Water Iris *(Iris virginica, I. laevigata, I. pseudacorus)*

Water iris vary in how much depth they prefer, and some species require a dry period in winter. However, if you consult with local water gardeners, you can surely find the right iris to grow within your water garden, or just outside its edges. Species vary in hardiness; the yellow flag *(L. pseudacorus)* shown here grows in Zones 5 to 8. In addition to the beautiful flowers, the fact that iris foliage contrasts beautifully with so many plants — and with stone — makes it a top choice for background plantings.

Water Clover (*Marsilea mutica*)

If four-leaved clovers bring luck, this is a fortunate plant to have, indeed. A floater with wandering roots that usually find suitable moorings in the pots of other aquatic plants, water clover is a fast grower in either sun or partial shade. Some selections are variegated with white or purplish bronze, and there is considerable variation in hardiness and species identification. They are rated for Zones 9 to 11, though I have wintered them over occasionally in Zone 7. Fortunately, they are easily replaced if lost.

Water Lotus (*Nelumbo* species)

One of the most ancient flowers to be appreciated by man, lotus remains a stately plant for any water garden that gets at least a half day of sun. Hardy varieties can survive to Zone 5, though the roots must not be allowed to freeze hard in winter. The plant shown here is *N. nucifera,* adapted to Zones 4 to 11. Look for newer varieties that rebloom, and grow them in submerged mud-filled pots. Lift and divide dormant tubers in early spring.

Water Lily (*Nymphaea* species)

Water lilies grow from submerged pots, produce leaves that float on the water's surface, and bloom again and again all summer long. Tropical varieties can be grown from Zone 8 southward, while some hardy hybrids are well adapted to Zone 4. To keep plants in bloom, fertilize several times during summer by tucking into the pots packets of fertilizer made from a half teaspoon of granular fertilizer 10-10-10 folded in a 6-inch square of paper towel. The cultivar shown here is 'St. Louis Gold'.

Water Lettuce (*Pistia stratiotes*)

Technically, water lettuce is a perennial, but it is not hardy except in Zones 10 to 11, and so it is treated as an annual elsewhere. Even though a water lettuce planting must be restocked yearly, the plants divide so quickly that they are inexpensive and widely available. A floater with long, threadlike roots, water lettuce provides excellent shelter for fish and helps keep water clean. The green rosettes keep their best color when they receive partial shade, particularly in the middle of the day.

CHAPTER 7

GARDEN ORNAMENTS

Some uses for stone incorporate yet transcend practical purposes, but to call them ornamental seems to fall short, too. Beautiful stones can hold containers captive, become irresistible places to sit,  or simply exist in the garden as the most elemental form of nature's art. When a well-figured stone stands as a sentinel between ornamental grasses and goldenrod, or a small boulder shields the base of an otherwise unguarded tree, stone enters the life of the garden at its deepest level.

Made formal by its sculptured supports, this stone bench echoes the line of the retaining wall behind it. Verbena, gayfeather, variegated dogwood, and other shrubs grow in the raised bed surrounding the sitting area.

Garden Stones for Sitting

Every landscape needs a special spot that is unusually quiet, sheltered, and serene, a place created especially for sitting. It may be where you go for solitude, removed from the world, or you may want to arrange things so you can accommodate company. The choice is yours, but I have noticed that gardeners who go to the trouble of handling sitting-sized stones are usually happiest if they do it just for themselves, placing sitting stones in the most private and personal places within the garden.

Of course, you can use a stone bench — or simply a stone block or boulder that's the right size for sitting — almost like a piece of sculpture in the garden. Stone benches tend to be reminiscent of significant stone monuments, perhaps even of Stonehenge, so they naturally draw attention. Sittable boulders are more like pleasant surprises, as are flat sitting surfaces built into stone walls or situated alongside steps. However, keep in mind that after one sees a stone sitting place of any kind, there is a natural pause during which we question whether or not that will really be a nice place to sit. If we take the leap and actually sit down, we will probably be just a little disappointed with its lack of comfort, because a stone seat does not compare well with a padded chair. It is therefore doubly important that, once you are seated on stone, the surrounding area be irresistibly appealing.

If you can't quite decide where to place a free-standing stone bench, look first for a place that gets morning sun and afternoon shade. In such a site, the stone will become warm and dry early in the day and be cool and inviting later, when you want an escape from afternoon heat.

Position a stone bench where it will get morning sun and afternoon shade. In such a site, the stone will become cool and inviting later, when you want to escape from afternoon heat.

There are no secrets to assembling a bench from base blocks and a top slab. The blocks must be firm and even, and the top must fit so well that it never wobbles. Because a slab large enough to sit on can weigh 200 pounds or more, you will need a helper to put it in place.

You can use single blocks, several layers of stacking stone, or a combination of the two to form the support blocks for a bench. You may even decide to use stone for the support posts and wood for the bench itself. The finished bench should be 16 to 18 inches from the ground, and you can estimate this height by measuring the thickness of the top slab — called the bench stone — and adding the height of the support blocks. Locate base stones so they will be 6 inches or so inside the edges of the bench stone. For extra stability, it's best to sink the base stones about 6 inches into the ground and then secure them in place with a mixture of gravel and soil, solidly tamped into place. Remember to consider the buried depth of the base stones when you are planning the height of your bench.

The rugged faces and impressive scale of the boulders form an interesting contrast to the highly polished wood of the Japanese-style bench that spans the space between them.

The two supports for your bench need not match. One might be a single block while the other is stacked stone, or both can be made of stacked stones of varying sizes. Indeed, if you are selecting stone from a large pile purchased primarily for other purposes, set aside possible base stones as you find them and experiment with ways of arranging them into solid supports. Use a board as a temporary seat, and you will have a good feel for your bench by the time you get to the hard part — placing the bench stone.

Two people working together can usually heft a bench stone onto its supports, but you may need a third person for the last step. Frequently, a bench stone won't fit perfectly, and you'll need to slide it around a bit or insert shims to stop small wobbles. If you don't have help at this stage, you can use a hydraulic jack placed under the middle of the bench stone to lift it very slightly. Place a board under the jack to keep it stable, and lift the bench stone only ¼ inch or so above the supports — just enough so you can pop in a shim stone where needed, or slide the bench stone forward or back until it's perfectly seated.

What Grows Beneath

The area beneath a bench can be covered with gravel, mulch, or pavers, and is an excellent spot to plant low-growing herbs like the Corsican mint (*Mentha requienii*) shown here. Surprisingly tough in spite of its somewhat delicate appearance, Corsican mint prefers moist soil in sun or part shade. Only ½ inch tall, this mint spreads freely over stones and releases a delightfully minty fragrance when walked on. In cold areas (Zone 5 and possibly even Zone 4) it dies back and resprouts in the spring, but it is evergreen in warmer areas. ∎

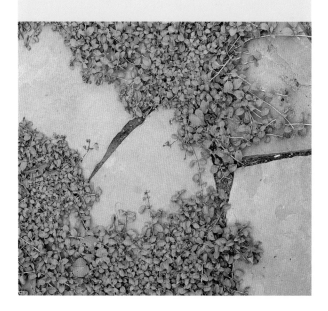

Benches Within Walls

If you want to create a sitting space within a stone wall, there are several ways to do it. If the wall is a retaining wall built into a slope, a sitting place will be instantly recognizable if you install a broad stone behind the bench that serves as both a visual and a practical backrest. This backrest can be made from several medium-sized flat stones rather than a single large one, but if you choose this technique, it's important that the stones fit together well and are secured at the corners with tie stones that are part of the adjoining wall. When piecing together several stones to form a backrest, try to make a clear, symmetrical pattern with the stones. The idea is to make this break in the wall look like a piece of furniture, so the backrest should mimic the design of the back of a sofa. Similarly, the bench stone can comprise three broad, flat stones rather than a single slab. Like the backrest, these stones should resemble sofa cushions in size and balance. If possible, have these sitting stones overhang the wall below them by at least an inch. Besides making sitting more comfortable, the small lip created by the sitting stones helps set them apart visually from the rest of the wall.

If you use a broad slab, you can make a wall bench even more inviting and dramatic. Decide where you want your bench within the wall and leave a break in the wall as you build it. Make the break as wide as the slab, minus 12 inches. This allows 6 inches on each end of the slab, which will be built into the wall as it nears the right height for sitting.

Massive stone slabs (ABOVE RIGHT) are artfully combined with slate accent pieces to create a stone bench that is more sculpture than it is garden furniture.

Bunchberry (Cornus canadensis) (RIGHT) is a creeping dogwood that is a good choice for cool, shady spots such as next to a stone bench.

You may use additional stones over the top edges of the slab as armrests, and flat stones behind the slab for a backrest. However, the open area beneath the slab makes it quite obvious that this is, indeed, a bench meant for sitting.

Sittable Boulders and Steps

Any boulder with a broad, flat top 14 to 18 inches above the ground can be considered a sitting stone, but it's important that the area around the boulder be landscaped in a way that makes sitting a clear part of the boulder's purpose. For example, the ground in front of the boulder needs to be level and paved with pebbles, stone, or mulch, and the area should have a feeling of enclosure, so that the boulder seems to be included in an outdoor room. A low wall or hedge behind the boulder can structure the enclosure, or you might install a threshold stone a few feet in front of the boulder to help separate the space from the rest of the landscape.

Similarly, whenever you build stone steps into a slope, you have an opportunity to add a seat or two to the plan. If a stone wall is to join one or both sides of the step, you can make an additional place to sit by topping off the wall with a single flat sitting stone.

Entry Accents

To the outside world, a gardener's talents are best displayed in the entryway — not only the first place visitors see but the scene you, too, encounter when you come home from a long day at work. Above all, an entryway should impart a strong sense of welcome, and there's no better way to do this than to make your entry as beautiful as possible. When used to structure or trim entryways, the solid presence of stone reassures all comers that their arrival has been anticipated, and the strength of stone deepens a feeling of safe passage.

When using stone to beautify entryways, keep in mind a few basic guidelines of landscape design. One invaluable concept, called the funnel effect, dictates that objects of any nature, including shrubs and structures made of stone, should decrease in size as one nears the entryway. The idea is to funnel the eye's attention toward the entryway, exaggerating perspective at the same time. When using stone, you might place large boulders or walls built of medium to large stones in the far reaches of your front yard, with stone of smaller size used in spaces closer to the door.

Small stone features near the entryway also work to carry out a pleasing sense of scale. For example, a massive stone pillar near a front door would easily overwhelm, whereas more diminutive touches, such as a bed framed with small stacking stone, blend much better with the little details present in entryways — doors, knobs and knockers, welcome mats, and small potted plants.

Streetside Stone

Many gardeners are challenged to come up with ways to coax guests into using the front door and walkway. If the front yard includes a slight slope, small curved retaining walls that frame the front walkway leave no question that the appropriate entry place has been reached. This type of stone feature works particularly well if the walls enclose a broad landing. People confidently conclude that such a wide, open spot is, indeed, where they should disembark from cars or begin their journey to your front door.

Depending on your taste, streetside walls can be planted or left bare in the interest of neatness. And because you are striving to create a place that feels

Sculptured stone (LEFT) is integrated into this entryway by a planting that includes conifers and cactus (*Opuntia humifusa*).

A streetside planting dominated by rough-cut boulders (TOP RIGHT) brings a taste of primitive nature to a suburban setting.

inviting, avoid plants that sprawl into walking areas, as well as those that attract bees and other buzzing insects. Ground covers and foliage plants are always safe bets, and they have the additional advantage of requiring little maintenance while keeping their handsome good looks over a very long season.

If your yard is smaller than your gardening aspirations, you may want to expand your cultivated space into walkway medians, those narrow strips between the sidewalk and the street. Check first to make sure this is legal in your town or neighborhood. If you decide to proceed, use softly rounded stones to edge your plantings. Besides providing a visual frame, stones keep plants from spreading into walking areas, protect them from trampling, and aid in drainage when rainwater flows over concrete walkways into the space you have planted.

Low-growing plants with fine texture are often the best candidates for planting in walkway medians. Dianthus, creeping phlox, sedums, and thymes carry out this assignment in grand style.

Keepsake Stones

Sooner or later, we all encounter special stones that make us sigh with pleasure each time we see them. It may be their shape or color, or the way lichen has etched a pretty pattern into the surface, or perhaps they represent fond memories of the places they were found. Look for spots near entryways to display such treasure stones. Tuck them into the mulch near plants that are especially dear to you, or find companion stones that can form a nest for the one you regard as the grandest jewel of your collection.

A favorite stone can be encircled with ivy and prominently displayed near an entryway.

Stone Lanterns

Because they are so beautiful, stone lanterns are often the first — and sometimes the only — purchased stone item added to a garden that is structured in natural stone. Yet stone lanterns have a long cultural and religious history well worth learning about, and certainly deserving of appreciation. Stone lanterns are much more than garden ornaments. Like stone water bowls (discussed on pages 201 and 201), stone lanterns are rich with symbolism. In small ways, they have contributed to the spiritual development of mankind for more than a thousand years.

In the gardens of Japan, stone lanterns serve as sentinels of light, yet they are used very differently from the way Western landscape designers use lampposts. Traditionally, Japanese stone lanterns are placed either by a turn in a path or near a bridge or series of stepping-stones that cross water. The use of light in these situations is both practical and symbolic. In addition to providing physical security and guidance for safe footing, the Japanese use of garden lighting to mark a change of direction or a crossing from one place to another is rich with spiritual symbolism that mirrors processes of inner growth. In a garden, stone lanterns emphasize these themes of passage both by day, with their structural form, and after dark, when they glow with soft light.

A stone lantern, tucked in among ferns and conifers, can indicate a turn in a path or access to a bridge across water.

Choosing a Lantern

Many upscale garden shops sell stone lanterns, which vary in price, depending on the stone from which they are made, the detail of the carving, and the lantern's size. Many are made from granite, which is considered the most traditional material, but you may fall in love with lanterns carved from sandstone or lava rock.

Don't be misled into paying a great deal extra for a lantern because of a claim that it has been hand-carved. This means simply that human beings manned the machines used to carve it. Instead, concentrate on the size and form of the lantern and choose one that is pleasing to you.

Some models include predrilled holes for electrical cords so that they can be easily outfitted with low-wattage bulbs that give off a soft glow. If the lantern isn't equipped with this feature, you can use a candle or a small oil or kerosene lamp to light it.

Very low, small lanterns, often called tabletop lanterns, can be set atop stone pedestals, blocks, or even stumps. Larger upright models stand alone as light-giving pillars, and they often are placed near water, where you can see their forms in reflection. Don't worry about not being able to handle very heavy lanterns. They come apart into pieces that two people can handle with ease.

If your climate is very cold or rainy, you may want a lantern with a broad roof that will capture snow and shed rain. Called snow-viewing lanterns (*yukimi-gama*), these garden ornaments can be very plain or quite ornate, and all are designed to show the purity of line that is made more dramatic with a soft blanket of snow.

Legacies of Tea

Both stone lanterns and water bowls are important elements in the traditional tea ceremony, a ritual practiced in Japan for hundreds of years. For the past 500 years, Tea has been used as a ritual that honors many of the values associated with Buddhism and Taoism — peace, consensus, harmony, respect, and humility. At several important points in Japanese history, military leaders brought together under the conciliatory influence of Tea were at last able to find the common ground they needed to establish peace.

The practice of the Japanese tea ceremony is an art form beyond the scope of this book, but the way that garden features such as lanterns and water bowls relate to tea ritual can be adopted by any gardener who wants to turn a special place into a peaceful oasis. Traditionally, that place would be a teahouse — a small, minimally furnished structure set apart from the rest of the garden. In your yard, it could be a quiet sitting area, a cool alcove beneath a tree, or a serene spot beside a water garden. Its only required characteristics are a sense of separateness and simple natural beauty, which combine to make it feel sacred.

The lantern is part of the approach to this special place of tranquillity. It helps lead the way, and it draws attention to the most dramatic part of the journey. A water bowl is a place for purification, where one rinses the dust of the world from hands and mouth. We'll look at ways to interpret this water ritual. Here, I wish to emphasize the symbolism that you might replicate by thoughtful placement of a stone lantern and water bowl in special places in your landscape. ■

Water Bowls

Since we are inhabitants of the water planet, it's only natural that we should want to include water in our gardens. If you don't have room for a pond or fountain (or even if you do), a stone water bowl can enrich your garden with the classic coolness of water.

Water bowls and basins may be reminiscent of ritual Japanese water bowls, but in Western landscape design, their use is usually completely ornamental. In gardens developed with wildlife in mind, shallow water bowls can double as birdbaths. Or you can fill them with smooth stones so that thirsty butterflies have a place to stand as they sip the sun-warmed water. Water bowls are too small to hold aquatic plants or fish, but when equipped with a small pump, they can accommodate a slow trickle of water that enriches the garden with its sparkle and sound.

You can carve a small water bowl out of sandstone (see page 210) or especially supple limestone, but it is faster to simply buy one. Or check your phone book to find a nearby maker of granite memorials. These professionals have beautiful stone and the proper equipment to create lovely, one-of-a-kind stone bowls.

Japanese Stone Water Bowls

The garden water basin is part of the traditional Japanese tea ceremony (explained on page 199). In Japan, Tea is a shared spiritual experience rather than simply a shared meal. Just before the guests arrive, the host fills the basin with fresh water, which may be carried in pails or delivered through a bamboo spout.

This traditional Japanese stone water bowl is constantly refreshed by water that flows from a bamboo spout housed in the rock wall above.

Then, before entering the teahouse, guests pause to wash their hands and rinse their mouths with cool water from a stone bowl. Stopping by the basin is a ritual act of cleansing, or purification, which prepares guests to participate in the tea ceremony.

To be authentic, such a water bowl should either be raised on a pedestal so that it is about 16 inches in height or be situated on the ground so that guests must kneel or squat to sink their hands into the water. The higher positioning is the more ancient tradition, but somewhere in history, tea masters lowered the acceptable height to emphasize the humility with which the tea ceremony should be approached. Today, the lower "crouching bowl," or *tsukubai*, is considered most proper for the tea ceremony.

Bamboo Fountains

You can use any type of fountain to deliver recirculated water to a stone bowl, but those made from bamboo are the most authentic. In a traditional Japanese bamboo fountain, called a *kakei,* an upright hollow bamboo pole is joined with a second piece that works as the outflow pipe. It is typically set 12 to 14 inches above the bowl. To prevent water loss, thread a piece of plastic pipe through the *kakei* as you assemble it. Underground, connect the plastic pipe to the outlet from the pump.

There are many other options for delivering recirculated water to a water bowl, such as including a cascade of stones at the rear of the bowl that looks like a miniature waterfall. To prevent water loss, install a short bamboo spout at the top of the fall so that the water does not hit stones until it has almost reached the bowl.

Recirculating Water

If you want the water in your basin to move, there are two approaches to consider. One is to set the bowl above a reservoir dug into the ground, with a small pump hidden in the reservoir. The water bowl itself can be situated at a very slight angle, so that water overflows its edge and flows into the reservoir below. Some bowls include a slight groove, cut into the top edge, that channels the overflow water into a small stream.

To support the water bowl over the reservoir, set the bowl atop two strong rebar stakes installed so that they span the top of the reservoir. Traditionally, the entire top of the reservoir is covered with a steel grate, with small stones arranged on top to hide the reservoir from view. However, many modern gardeners want to see as much water as possible, so they use stone to dress the edges of the reservoir and camouflage the rebar stakes, but they leave the sides of the reservoir, on either side of the bowl, in clear sight.

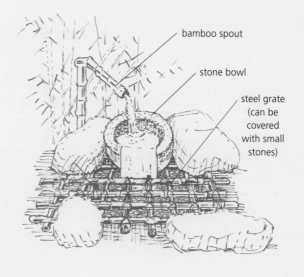

bamboo spout

stone bowl

steel grate (can be covered with small stones)

Whimsical Additions

Gardeners may sometimes seem to be narrowly focused, plant-obsessed sorts of people. But many of them have creative urges that lead them to pursue unique projects that blend diverse interests involving plants, stone, and one or more additional wild cards. These are the gardeners most likely to slather a wood birdhouse with mortar and stud it with small pebbles, or paint faces on flat, smooth stones, or perhaps stack a small wall to provide a suitable sitting place for scarecrows.

It's an obsessive process, in which an idea takes root and begins to grow once you've found the seed. At Rock City, near Chattanooga, Tennessee, one gardener began years ago to collect native plants to grow in the nooks and crannies of Lookout Mountain. Eventually, gnomes began to appear, and now this major tourist attraction blends stone, plants, and hundreds of fairy-tale figures.

Live animals are seldom safe to keep in a garden, which may be why so many of us feel compelled to import artificial versions. These may be concrete statues of rabbits or frogs; giant ants or butterflies made out of twigs, wood, or metal; topiary elephants; or even dinosaurs if you want to evoke the feel of the prehistoric. The right stones can help set the mood. In one garden I visited, for example, a group of concrete sheep nibbling grass was transformed into an appropriate alpine scene by shallow stones set into the ground around them. The stones had a dwarfing effect on the grass, so that it required less mowing and appeared naturally shorn. A smaller scene that charmed me involved a singular concrete duck that had been given its own narrow stone walkway among some hydrangeas. The little walkway was only a few inches wide, but it made all the difference between a duck statue stuck in a garden and the pleasurable illusion that a happy duck called the place home.

These are but two examples of using stone to create an imaginary habitat for an animal figure — the secret to breathing life into animal statuary in the garden. Frogs and turtles are logical choices to place near water features, while a desert scene would be a natural place to encounter an iguana. When well placed, animal figures in the garden quickly become companionable presences, and many gardeners go so far as to bestow names upon their beloved friends.

Garden Railroads

Built on a scale that matches the train, garden railroads are increasingly popular specialty gardens. Local garden railroad clubs throughout North America can be easily located on the Web, a great way to get started with this fascinating hobby. Stone is always an integral part of the miniature world of a railroad garden. It provides visual touch points to define scale, creates picturesque mountains and tunnels, and even echos the sounds of whistles as the train clacks its way down the track. ■

The use of stone statuary has a long tradition in garden design. Each of the stone ornaments on the opposite page achieves its effect in a different way — whether through surprise, whimsy, or a nod to antiquity.

The Art of Placing Stones

The most elemental — and often most dramatic — use of stone in the garden presents stones just as they are, with no practical function or enveloping foliage to distract you from contemplating their timeless textures. Stones that are partially buried can become upright sentinels. Rocks and boulders of unusual color or shape can be placed in mysterious configurations in unexpected spots.

For the more practical uses of stone, such as walls and steps, it is best to stick with common local varieties. This is partly so that your construction blends into the landscape and partly because it is more affordable. When you are placing stones for artistic effect, on the other hand, you have a chance to make use of the most interesting and unusual stones you have collected.

Scattered Stones

Once you make stone a primary element in your garden, you will find few places where stones do not belong. Little ones with interesting textures or colors are often the perfect finishing touches for plants grown in containers, and even large stones that you run across while building bigger projects will often beg to be set aside for display in some prominent place. One of my recent finds is a flat piece of limestone I had intended to use as paving. The fossils embedded in the surface are so intricate that nothing

In a garden designed for contemplation, a stump filled with balanced stones poses mysterious questions (LEFT).

A series of thin, jagged stones suggest the remains of a rustic wooden fence (ABOVE RIGHT).

will do but to prop it up in a place where it can be closely studied with both eyes and fingertips. Because ferns are part of the picture nature has etched in the limestone, placing the stone among ferns will be like returning it to its home.

When I walk in the woods, I am often amused by the places in which nature manages to put small stones — in tree crotches, squeezed between knotty roots, or simply scattered about willy-nilly, in places that defy explanation in terms of gravity, wind, or water. They are homeless stones, no longer associated with their parent rocks, left to weather and gather moss and simply be what they are.

But a yard is a domesticated space, so it's best if there is some rhyme or reason to where orphan stones are placed. This is a game you can make up as you go along. Small egg-shaped stones can be given an appropriate nest. Stones that have cracked in two can be planted or propped so that the fissure seems to have happened only a moment before, leaving one to wonder over the forces that cause such events. Long cylindrical stones can be planted in the garden, like rockets ready for takeoff. Bury broken geodes along a pathway's edge so that only their glossy hearts can be seen. The goal of this game is a simple one: to help every stone belong.

Obviously positioned in this man-made setting of informal flooring and water-loving plants at the Innisfree Garden, this monolithic stone, with its primitive ruggedness, is unsettling.

Planting Stones

Extremely large boulders can be set into slight depressions dug into the ground, but unless a stone is truly massive, it should be "planted" so that about one-third of it is buried. Planted stones not only look more natural but also are much more stable than stones set on the ground. When you plant stones securely, they will not shift out of position, altering the lines of your composition.

To help envision exactly where you want to place a group of large stones, stuff garbage bags with crumpled newspaper and use them as dummies for your layout. Use white bags for light-colored stones and black ones for boulders that are dark in color. If you are setting out container-grown plants as you set large stones in the ground, go ahead and buy them, and arrange them around the dummy bags to get a clear idea of how the finished garden will look.

Once you've decided on placements, begin "planting" stones at the lowest levels first. Measure the stone to be planted, and then dig a hole for it about 6 inches wider than the base of the stone. Avoid digging too deep, because you want the stone

to sit on compacted subsoil. Before placing the stone in the hole, study it carefully so that you will know precisely the surfaces and angles you want to see aboveground. Once the stone is in the hole, use pry bars and shim stones to get it exactly the way you want it. When planting an upright stone, brace it with scrap lumber until you can backfill and firmly tamp the soil around it. Unless the soil right around the stone is destined to become a home for plants, it's a good idea to include gravel or rubble stone in the soil used as backfill. When you're finished, pack it all in as firmly as you can.

Single Specimen Stones

When used solo, upright specimen stones offer an unmatched opportunity to partner stones with plants, call attention to special views, or simply announce to the world that you honor the permanence of stone. To make sure that upright stones stay straight, plant them as deeply as you can. Large specimen stones with broad, heavy bases may require only shallow planting.

Prepare holes for plants when you install the stones. If the stone is to be the focal point, avoid plants that will overpower it, such as evergreen trees or rampant vines. Also, keep in mind that once a large stone is planted, it's much easier to change companion plants than to move the stone.

A cut boulder (ABOVE LEFT) reveals the natural layers within the stone, as well as the marks of the tools used to divide it. Strappy daylily leaves echo the graceful lines.

A slender stone pillar in a rustic yet sculptural shape (ABOVE RIGHT) is hugged closely by climbing vines, such as summer-flowering clematis.

Stone Cairns

Historically, a cairn was a conical pile of stones used to commemorate a sacred site or place of burial. Thousand-year-old cairns can be found throughout the British Isles, particularly in Scotland, often in combination with Stonehenge-type monuments.

In the garden, a small cairn can mark a turn in the path, or it can be a beautiful, unexpected focal point. Extremely easy to create, a cairn is an excellent use for small stone left over from other projects. You can also build a cairn gradually by adding interesting stones to it as you discover them. Even a garden sculpture as simple as three stacked stones can contribute not only an aesthetic touch but also a sense of serenity and permanence to a quiet corner of the garden. ■

Stone Groupings

A group of planted stones can subtly indicate the direction that visitors should travel when passing through a garden. You might also place a grouping at a stopping point to add a sculptural feature for contemplation.

When placing a group of stones, consider how the distances between individual stones affects your composition. Stones that are too far apart appear unrelated; a carefully considered distance can create an almost gravitational tension between stones.

Another possibility is to place a series of small stones so that they imitate larger stone walls or perhaps the opening of a cave or passageway. These stones can be matched with plants to create the illusion of a hidden place to picnic, read, or simply rest for a moment.

Changes through the Seasons

A garden still life composition may be still for a moment, but it changes with the seasons. The stone element is the constant; it may be accompanied by evergreens and tree bark in winter, fresh new foliage in spring, colorful flowers in summer, and newly fallen leaves in autumn. Some evergreen presence is always needed, either as part of the composition itself or as a dark backdrop for the entire scene. Light-colored stone appears lighter against an evergreen backdrop, and winter never seems quite so dead when splashes of green are present.

When working primarily with shrubs and trees, look for cultivars with multiseason interest or long bloom times. Trees with weeping habits always attract attention, and shrubs that feature colorful foliage and a long parade of flowers (such as Japanese spirea) or berries (such as many viburnums) are hard to beat when they work side by side with stone. Many gardeners find that one plant with bronze-red foliage really brings a still life to life, particularly where stone is involved.

From a practical point of view, you may find that stone is most needed on the ground. To make it easier to visit a little snowbell or dwarf apricot tree in full bloom, a gravel and stepping-stone walkway may be needed. Or if a butterfly bush is in the picture, you may need a stone upon which to stand as you deadhead the flowers.

Obviously, growing a garden still life is more complicated than simply arranging fruit in a bowl on a table, but it's a project that you can enjoy for many years, season after season.

Stones planted on both sides of a gradually narrowing opening (LEFT) lead one inward to a special hideaway.

Flowering trees enjoy the year-round company of stones at their bases (NEAR RIGHT).

Junipers below the rocks (FAR RIGHT) will still provide color in this spot even when the leaves of the Japanese maple have fallen.

Carving Stone

Once stone gets in your blood, it's natural to consider carving as yet another way to enrich your life with stone. Stone carving is an art in itself, and what you can do depends on what types of stone you have to work with and what you hope to accomplish. I shall assume that you don't want to get involved with expensive diamond cutters or sandblasting tools, and simply want to do a little hand carving with tools that are powered by muscle rather than electricity. Even with these limits, there are several projects worth considering if you can get your hands on the right kind of stone.

Sculpting Stone

Most of the stone used for building is too hard or irregular for shaping into sculpture without power tools. However, you may be able to sculpt a shallow bowl if you're willing to spend many hours chipping away at a block of limestone with a rock hammer and chisel. I've been doing this myself for several months, whenever I'm in the mood to bang away on my limestone bowl. It's slow work, indeed, but there is a certain satisfaction in making a half inch of progress on a good day.

Sandstone is a much softer stone, and the right type is not difficult to carve into a bowl or a planter. However, you will need a block that has a light, soft texture and an even grain, with few striations, as well as a special carving tool called a toothed scutch. This tool is like a chisel with a toothed blade at the end, which is replaced as it becomes dull. The teeth bite into stone much better than a plain chisel, but you may need to look hard to find this rare tool.

To make more elaborate sculptures without using power tools, it's worth the trouble to locate and buy a piece of soapstone. This soft stone can be sculpted with hand chisels and smoothed with sandpaper, but the best pieces come from Africa and South America. Several companies on the Web offer raw soapstone blocks by mail.

Carved Rock Art

Long before people had access to steel chisels, they carved art into stone. In the soft sandstones of Minnesota and Kansas, Native Americans carved figures of people and animals using chisels made of harder stone or antlers, struck with flat hammer stones. You can do this today if you have soft sandstone to work with, but the right kind of stone is absolutely essential. You will also need a fine-tipped chisel and plenty of patience, because even a primitive carving cannot be done in a day.

This is a project to go at spiritually, with a certain degree of reverence. It is believed that most of the carved petroglyphs of the Midwest were carved by

Starting with small blocks of soapstone, figures like these whimsical fish can be carved with hand tools.

shamans, who sought to express deep meanings about life and survival, or perhaps conjure magic with their carvings in stone. Keep your design simple, and be mindful that carving is an ancient way to teach a stone to speak.

Pecked Petroglyphs

Much of the aboriginal stone art of the Southwest and the Northeast is pecked into stone rather than actually carved. This is a craft you can undertake with any type of stone that is a different color only ⅛ to ¼ inch under the surface. For example, the petroglyphs of Maine are pecked into gray shale that has a thin coating of rust-colored volcanic rock. In the Southwest, petroglyphs are pecked into any type of stone covered with desert varnish, including superhard basalt.

You can use a fine-tipped chisel and small rock hammer to peck a relief pattern in suitable stone. It is important to be patient and work slowly, because a design can quickly be ruined by chipping off flakes in just the wrong place.

Messages in Stone

The stones sold at garden and gift shops bearing words or phrases always claim to be hand carved, which means that a person operated the machinery used to engrave the stones. These often make interesting additions to a stone-encrusted landscape when situated in just the right spot, but stones need not bear words to impart their messages. As shown throughout this chapter, there are endless ways to stack, place, or balance stones so that they enrich your garden with structure, meaning, and fun. With your own creativity as your guide, there is no end to the ways you can use stone to help your garden tell its own unique story.

The Mount Rushmore Mystique

Mount Rushmore in South Dakota is carved out of granite, but don't get the idea that it was done by hand. The initial roughing out required dynamite, and then hundreds of workers operating jackhammers took over. Even with all that labor, completing the sculpture took more than six years. So it's not the kind of thing you can expect to do in your backyard. ■

A simple water bowl carved from a sandstone block makes a delightful garden ornament.

CHAPTER 8

WORKING WITH STONE

Stonework, even more than other garden tasks, must be approached slowly, mindfully, and with safety always in mind. In this look at the practical side of working with stone, I've included many  things I've discovered the hard way. But the main thing I've learned over the years is that if you work carefully and pay attention, the stone itself can help you set the right pace and find its best use, and your results may far exceed your initial expectations.

A study in contrasts, this informal stepping-stone path combines rounded stones in a seemingly endless palette of sizes, shapes, colors, and textures.

Getting Started with Stone

Gardeners are used to hard work — digging holes, pulling weeds, and spreading mulch — but many find the prospect of working with heavy, unyielding stone a little intimidating. There is one wonderful aspect of adding stone to your garden, however: Once stonework is finished, it is really and truly done. Today's labor becomes tomorrow's beauty, which becomes even more enthralling as garden stones and plants settle in to share one another's company.

To get the most enjoyment from working with stone, I think it's crucial to pay attention to pacing. You don't want to push your body to do more heavy lifting than it can handle, and by working slowly, you give your brain the time it needs to give lifting challenges the care they deserve. I have also found that the more I get to know individual stones, often in the process of transporting them, the more satisfied I am with the way I use them in my garden.

Gathering Stone

Almost every gardener I know who has adopted stone as a key garden element began the same way. We began noticing stones as we visited different places, found ourselves tucking special stones into the trunks of our cars, and soon accumulated a small pile of personal treasure rocks. Then one day the light popped on: We could have *more* stone, possibly all that we wanted and needed, and we could use it to make our gardens exactly the way we felt they should be.

A lovingly crafted old stone wall becomes more beautiful as it weathers and ages and more plants poke from its crevices.

Save Their Skins

Naturally, you will want to preserve the art that nature has etched in stones in the form of lichens or moss, and it's important to protect bare stone from scuffs and scratches as well. The outer surface of weathered stone is usually quite different from the rock inside, and a bad scrape will take many years to weather away.

If you're working with a large specimen stone, it's wise to wrap it in old blankets, carpet padding, or furniture padding tied securely with rope before you move it. Leave the wrapping on until just before the stone is placed in its final position. At that point, wrap your pry bars with cloth to keep from scratching the stone as you move it into its place.

Should an abrasion appear in just the wrong place anyway, commit to some creative thinking to see how you can repair the damage. A slurry of peat moss, water, and a little ground charcoal rubbed into the scratch may stain it at least temporarily, or you might see if you can use a vine or other type of plant to hide the injury from view. ■

This is an exciting turn in the creativity road, and it's one where we often think we must choose between collecting and buying stone. Yet you don't have to choose one or the other; you can do both. Buying is usually simpler, and if you need large amounts of stone, you will probably end up buying the bulk of it. However, always be on the lookout for collecting possibilities and for unique sources of stone. This process often resembles a scavenger hunt.

Recently, I noticed a block in my town where the Victorian homes are being lovingly restored, one by one. In two yards I saw stone benches that I admired, and I decided to try to track down their source. After knocking on doors, I was told of a nearby farm "that grows stone benches." It was then easy to find the farm family who had developed a cottage industry of trimming limestone blocks and slabs for benches — an invaluable resource for gardeners like me who want a stone bench without taking on the job of cutting 200-pound pieces in the proper shape.

By the way, don't think that you're intruding by asking gardeners about their stonework. Gardeners are generous people, and they love to share stone stories, almost like fishermen enjoy talking about the big one that got away. So whether you buy stone, collect it, or both, always remember that gardeners who have already stacked a few tons of stone are among your best sources of advice.

Shopping for Stone

Dealers who sell stone are perfectly aware that stone that is nicely faced with two or more flat sides, in just the right size for handling by a human being, is much more valuable than rougher stuff that must be cut or trimmed before it can be used. One gardener I know discovered that if he hand-selected the stones he wanted, the price of the load doubled. He wasn't happy at first, but then he got his chosen stone home and started using it to build a pond and several large raised beds. He had to trim only a few stones, and he decided that hand-selected stone was worth its cost.

In my first big adventure with stone, I bought three tons of stacking stone, though my estimates suggested that I needed only two. I was buying out of a huge bin rather than buying pre-selected stone on pallets, so I knew that much of the stone would not be worthy of walls. This turned out to be a wise move, though I eventually used every last stone. Stones that were not flat enough to use for my walls worked quite well for framing tree wells, and I used much of the rubble as backfill.

The bottom line is that if you're hand-selecting stone, you'll pay more but get exactly what you want. If you're not hand-selecting, the stone costs less, but you should buy about one-third more than you think you'll need for your primary projects.

The Ashfield Stone Company in western Massachusetts offers customers a wide variety of sizes and shapes to choose from. Be sure to research stone suppliers near you to find the best possible selection of stone.

Estimating Amounts

How much stone you will need depends on numerous factors, so there are no hard and fast rules that will tell you how much to buy. It's best to plan your project in detail, complete with a rough drawing, and take it with you when you go to buy stone. For example, a low retaining wall 18 inches high and 20 feet long requires about 1 ton of well-faced stacking stone. However, unless every last stone is usable, which is very unlikely, you will need a little extra. And if the stones are mostly large and thick, you will likely need a little more weight as well, because it takes only a few large stones to make up a ton.

With paving stone, it's easier to estimate how much you will need, as long as you have a good measurement of the square footage you plan to cover. Paving stone is usually loaded onto pallets, so first count how many layers of stone the pallet holds. Then measure the surface area of the pallet and whip out your calculator to figure the square footage. Finally, multiply the number of layers by the square footage to get the total square foot coverage of the pile.

Let the stone contractor help you with your estimates, too. Professionals are usually in the business of installing stone in addition to selling it, so they have plenty of firsthand experience in estimating amounts for various projects. Don't forget to ask if additional stone of the same type is likely to be available should you need more. The answer is usually yes, but you certainly don't want to start on a project, run out of stone, and not be able to get more that matches.

Plan on at least two trips to the stoneyard: one to survey what's available so you can budget your money, and a return trip to make your final selection and close the deal. If you buy more than three tons, delivery costs often become quite affordable.

Finding Free Stone

The best variety of stone to add to your garden, of course, is the kind you don't have to pay for. Here are some possible sources of free stone:

▶ **Construction sites.** Places where new roads, houses, or other buildings are being built are often good sources of stone. Stop by when construction crews are at work and see if you can get permission to gather the stone that you want. Then go back in the evening or on a weekend to load up, so that you won't get in the way of the workers.

▶ **Fields.** If you live in a farming area, be on the lookout for plowed fields that seem to have lots of stone scattered in the soil. Chances are good that any farmer plagued with stony soil has a stockpile you can pick through with his or her blessing.

▶ **Public land.** National forests and other public lands that are logged periodically may yield up good stone, but you'll need to know where to go to gather it legally. Check with the closest Forest Service office, or find a listing for the Bureau of Land Management. Tell them what you want, and you may be directed to wonderful sources near roads that have recently been graded or areas that have just been logged.

A REMINDER: Don't gather stone from public parks or green spaces intended for all to enjoy. Like wildflowers, stone is part of the natural scenery and should never be pilfered. ■

If you live near a quarry, you may be able to buy cut stone for special paving projects or have stone cut to your measurements. Handle cut stone carefully, because it's easily broken and can have sharp edges.

Room to Maneuver

For the past six months, I have been watching some homeowners build a large stone wall in their front yard, complete with a gigantic mistake. When the site was prepared, they had a bulldozer push several large boulders out of the way so they could build the wall. Now the boulders need to be moved or at least repositioned, but access to them is blocked by the new wall. It's an expensive lesson to learn, and I pass it on in the hope that you'll remember that access is everything when it comes to moving large stones. You don't want to have to go one step out of your way if you're moving them yourself, and any large equipment hired to help must have ample room to work.

Never lose sight of two basic facts about stone. First, stone is always easiest to move downhill. Second, stone is much easier to drag or roll than to lift and carry. ■

Bringing Stone Home

If you buy stone in sufficient quantity, the contractor may deliver it free of charge. Or if you have a pickup truck, you can carry it home yourself, one ton at a time. Stone that is already stacked on pallets will be lifted into your truck with a forklift, assuming the pallet fits. Otherwise, you'll need to load it into your truck by hand.

Whether you haul it yourself or have it delivered, plan in advance where you will stockpile your stone. Ideally, this spot should be as close to the construction site as possible. Make sure that someone is home to tell the driver where to put the load, since the supplier is otherwise likely to simply dump it out of the back of the truck. Stories abound of gardeners who come home from work to find their stone in the middle of their driveway, completely blocking entrance to the garage. It's also smart to cover the ground with plywood before the truck arrives. The plywood will protect the ground, while keeping the stone clean of dirt and mud.

If you unload stone yourself, you can sort it into piles as you take it off the truck. Set aside large square stones that would make good cornerstones, extra-thick stones you might use for the base of a wall, and particularly beautiful flat stones for paving. Make a separate pile of small, unremarkable stones. Although you may not realize it at the time, your brain is making notes on individual stones, and once you start stacking, you will remember seeing just the stone you need. Sorting stones into piles of similar types will make these special stones easier to find when you need them.

Moving Large Stones

Even if you never cut or trim a single stone, you will definitely have to move some. Whether you are lifting and stacking or pushing, pulling, and rolling large stones into place, always respect the weight of stone. In my very first stone project — a raised bed framed with large river rocks — I forgot to let go of a big one as I dropped it into place. I never thought that my littlest finger could provoke so much pain! Luckily for me, no bones were broken as I learned this important first lesson in moving stone: Always move slowly and thoughtfully when working with stone.

Heavy gloves will protect your hands from the abrasion that's part of handling stone, but it's important to wear heavy boots, too. After your hands, your toes are the body part next most vulnerable to injury, followed closely by your back.

Don't hesitate to make use of the stone-moving methods described on the next pages to keep from straining your back, and also practice proper lifting form (see box, above right). But most important, don't attempt to lift stones that are simply too heavy. Instead, get help, the proper tools, or both.

Finally, moving and stacking stone is heavy work, so be sure to take frequent breaks and stop work for the day when exhaustion sets in. Pushing yourself too hard will take the joy out of the process and increase your risk of painful accidents.

Lifting Heavy Weights

The proper way to lift any heavy weights, including stones, is to keep your knees bent and your back straight, so that you do most of the lifting with the strong muscles of your thighs and shoulders, rather than your back. For better leverage, keep the weight you're lifting as close to your body as possible. ■

Newly built walls tend to look stark and raw. By setting plants as you build, the scene quickly becomes more natural looking.

Twelve Ways to Move Stone

Decide which of the following methods to use based on the individual stone's size and shape and how far it must be moved. Should you find that the task you have undertaken is beyond your strength or abilities, either get help or give it up. Even though moving stone is hard work, it should be just a little bit fun, too.

A word of caution: Moving large boulders is not a job for amateurs, because it is best done with heavy equipment. Contractors who routinely handle boulders usually do so with a crane, which lifts multiton stones in a sling and gently sets them in place. Bulldozers or bobcat loaders often are used to move and place smaller boulders, and to dig the holes where large boulders will be planted. Let the experts handle this heavy work, and make it your job to provide a detailed plan for the placement of huge stones. If your landscape plan calls for boulders, have them installed before you begin building smaller projects in stone. The methods below are invaluable for moving small to medium-sized stones once you have collected them or had them delivered to your yard.

Dragging stones. When you use techniques for dragging stone, you expend less energy than you would by defying gravity to pick them up. However, because stones have no handles, it's easiest to place them on something that does. It's surprisingly easy to move large flat stones by placing them across an old tire and then dragging the tire. You can use a rope tied to the tire or hook a hoe or spade into the rim of the tire and drag it by pulling on the tool handle.

A friend found that heavy-duty plastic storage bins are good for moving stone, too. Because their bottoms are smooth, they are easy to push down a slope, or you

can drag them along with a hoe or shovel hooked into the rim. When you get where you're going, simply dump out the bin.

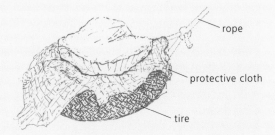

rope

protective cloth

tire

Stone sled. In the old days, when entire buildings were often made of stone, stonemasons used heavy-duty sleds to transport stone. Few of us move stone in such quantity that a stone sled is a worthwhile investment, but you can still use an old sled to move stone. Outfit the bottom with a piece of plywood, and replace flimsy rope handles with strong nylon cord or straps. Be careful when moving a sled loaded with stone down a slope, because it can easily get out of control. The other disadvantage of using a sled is that it can cause serious damage to grass.

wooden frame

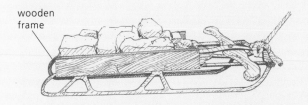

Mechanic's dolly. The same type of flat-wheeled dolly mechanics use to slide under your car can be used to move stone, particularly over a level paved surface. You can build one yourself by attaching wheels to a simple wood frame, or you may be able to borrow one first, to see how you like working with it. Tie on a rope, load it up, and pull the stone to where you need it. Be careful on a slope, because this kind of dolly can take off fast once it's loaded with heavy stone.

If you're working on a slope, consider making a simple two-wheeled dolly from a piece of scrap plywood. Install two screw-in, ball-type wheels at one end of a ¾-inch-thick piece of plywood (18 by 24 inches is a good size), and cut a hole in the opposite end large enough to attach a tow rope. It's also a good idea to nail a short piece of wood along the back end of the dolly (the end with wheels), to keep stones from sliding off. If a two-wheeled dolly starts getting away from you, dropping the tow rope usually brings it to a halt.

Garbage can. Heavy-duty trash receptacles equipped with two wheels make good stone-moving devices as long as you don't overload them. Lay them on their sides to push in a few stones, and then tip them up and wheel them to your building site. Lay them back down for easy unloading.

wheels down on ground

Ball-cart. A ball-cart, sometimes called a basket dolly, is easier to use than either a wheelbarrow or a garden cart, because the stone does not need to be lifted — only walked, pivoted, or levered into the basket of the cart. Nurserymen use ball-carts to move balled-and-burlapped trees, and you can sometimes find them to rent. Rounded stones can usually be rolled into the basket of a ball-cart, or you can use a pry bar to help lift a flat stone onto its end before pivoting it into the basket.

If you're determined and creative, a ball-cart is among the best ways to move stone up a slope. Load the stone

you want into the ball-cart, tie it in place with ropes or bungee cords, and then use a come-along or winch to pull the loaded cart up the hill. This works best with two people working — one to operate the lifting device and one to guide the loaded ball-cart.

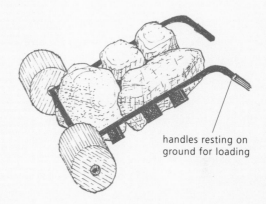

handles resting on ground for loading

Wheelbarrow. Any sturdy wheelbarrow can be used to move stone. Avoid loading a wheelbarrow so that it's heavy in the front, even though putting most of the weight toward the back will make it harder to lift. If there's too much weight up front, over the wheel, it's harder to keep the thing balanced. When using a wheelbarrow to move stacking stone, it's far better to carry many small loads than to try to maintain control of an overloaded wheelbarrow.

When using a wheelbarrow to move larger stones, attempt to move only one at a time, and get a helper to assist getting the stone in and out of the wheelbarrow. This is best done by laying the wheelbarrow on its side next to the stone, rolling or tipping the stone into the tub, and having one person pull on the top side of the wheelbarrow while the other pushes on the stone. Once the wheelbarrow is upright, take a moment to reposition the stone so that it is as well balanced as possible. To unload the stone, one person should support the stone while the other gently tips the wheelbarrow on its side. Then use a pry bar or planks and rollers to move the stone into place.

Pry bars and planks. It's beyond me why every time I go to the flea market to look for tools, there are lots of long-handled pry bars available for only a few bucks. I suppose they used to be more popular, or perhaps people buy them to use once, and then they sit around gathering dust. This is fortunate for us stone gardeners, because it's good to have two pry bars, at least 4 feet long, to lift stones that are half buried or to raise big paving stones that are lying on the ground. Like magic, the lever power of a pry bar far exceeds what you can do by working your fingers under a stone and pulling upward. A short pry bar, like those used as tire tools, just won't do the job. For lifting heavy stones, you will need a longer pry bar for sufficient power.

To increase the lever power of a pry bar, you can place a small block of wood behind it, which works as a fulcrum, making it possible to lift the edge of the stone with the curved end of the pry bar at least 2 inches off the ground. Once an edge of a stone is pried up, slip the end of a wood plank under it to keep it aloft. Then you can pry up another edge and shove in another plank. Any stout piece of lumber will do for this job, and you may be able to use scrap pieces from construction sites. Home supply stores always keep a cart of odds and ends, too, including scuffed pieces of oak or other hardwoods that stay nice and stiff under the weight of heavy stones. After your stone is up and ready to be moved to where you want it, use one of the other methods described here.

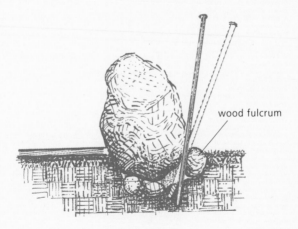

wood fulcrum

Planks and rollers. The ancient Egyptians used rollers to move the massive stone blocks that make up the pyramids — and rollers remain a fine way to move large stones. But we can be a little more sophisticated: Add planks to the setup. Smooth rollers, such as short lengths of metal pipe, combined with smooth planks make using this method simple. However, it's still easiest when two people work together, with one pushing the stone while the other manages the rollers.

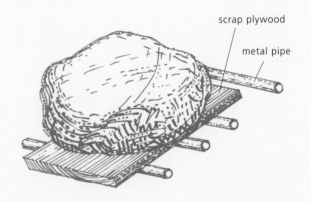

scrap plywood

metal pipe

A double-plank setup that rolls over four pieces of pipe works best, because it eliminates the complications posed by uneven ground. Lay a piece of scrap plywood over the area to be traversed, right next to the stone. Place a smaller piece of scrap wood over the base plank, and put a wedge-shaped stone between the two planks on the side farthest from the stone. Insert two or three pieces of pipe next to one another along the crevice created by the wedge, and then use a pry bar (or two) to work the stone onto the top of the upper plank. Have a helper steady the stone while you remove the wedge and replace it with the last piece of pipe. Then work together to rock the stone onto the top plank and get it rolling. Slowly roll the upper plank until it moves beyond the first piece of pipe, and stop long enough to move the freed pipe to front position. This procedure may feel awkward at first, but you'll soon get the hang of it. Naturally, when you reach the end of the base plank, you'll need another one to continue on your way.

Garden cart. Two-wheeled garden carts, including the kind you push or pull by hand and the type you can pull behind a lawn tractor, are great for moving large stones over reasonably smooth terrain. Or, if you can find one for rent, one of the new motorized carts is great for moving heavy stone. The only precaution with carts is that with two wheels to balance them, once they are heavily loaded, they can get away from you and take off down a hill.

Loading a large stone onto a cart can usually be done by setting the cart on its end next to the stone and using a board or pry bar to shift the stone onto the gate of the cart. It's a good idea to place a piece of scrap carpeting under the gate at the back of the cart first, so that as the cart is lifted, a helper can pull on the carpet to help ease the stone into the cart. The carpet also makes it possible to unload the stone by removing the gate and rolling the stone directly to where you want it to go.

Straps and winch. The same kind of winch used to pull a boat onto a trailer can be used to pull a heavy stone. Tow trucks are usually equipped with motorized winches, but a motorized winch is useless unless it's securely mounted on a vehicle. A manual winch needs a secure mounting, too, but if you already have one on a boat trailer, you can probably use it to move a big stone. Of course, you will first need to tie up the stone securely with nylon straps or rope, and provide wood planks or a ramp if you are dragging the stone over the ground. And, although I've never seen it done, I would not be reluctant to try using a winch to support a loaded garden cart or ball-cart being worked up a hill.

Chains and come-along. If you have some experience with working a come-along, consider using one to pull large stones across your yard, or even up a hill. The advantage of this device is that it's portable, and with the help of ropes or chains, you can attach a come-along to a tree or truck, and then crank the come-along to inch the stone to where it is needed. However, this is very slow work, and by the time you've set up your rigging and relocated a stone or two, half the day may be gone. However, if you

have a couple of lovely stones in one part of your yard that you want to move elsewhere, several hours working with a come-along combined with planks and rollers beneath the stones may be time very well spent.

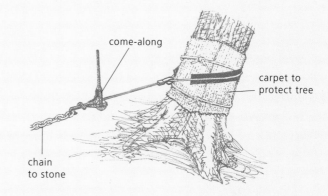

come-along

carpet to protect tree

chain to stone

Pry bar and ropes. After you've placed a large stone approximately where you want it to go, you can use pry bars tied to the stone with ropes to pivot and wiggle it into place. This is the method you will need to use when "planting" large specimen stones in an upright position, or when arranging a group of large stratified stones so that their layers all line up in the same direction.

Take the time to study the knotting system pictured here, as you will basically use ropes to weave a loose basket around the stone, with pry bars (or long wood dowels or tool handles) tied on to use as handles. Be sure that you don't tie the ropes so that they end up under the stone, even if you must stop and rearrange your ropes and knots. It's better to work slowly and thoughtfully than to get frustrated by trying to go too fast.

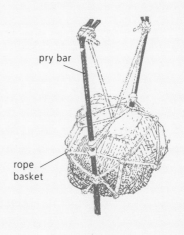

pry bar

rope basket

Cutting and Trimming Stone

The procedure for cutting sandstone used for paving is described on page 53, and smooth sandstone is the easiest type to trim. However, you may need to cut or trim other types of stone when building walls, steps, or benches, and the difficulty of this operation depends on the hardness and grain of the stone. Generally, it's best to cut and trim as little as possible, both because it's hard to do and because cut edges look barren and unnatural compared with weathered stone surfaces.

Two primary tools are needed to trim stone — a heavy mason's hammer, which has a head that's flat at one end and pointed at the other, and a cold chisel. I have found good selections of mason's hammers at flea markets, I suppose because a good one will last forever, provided it is not left out in the weather. However, I suggest buying a new 1-inch cold chisel, because recently manufactured ones are equipped with a hard plastic guard that protects your hands in the event that you miss your mark when you whack the chisel. This feature is well worth the extra cost of buying this tool new. If you are trimming a lot of thick stone, you will probably need a wider cold chisel as well, such as one with a 2- or 3-inch-wide blade.

Stone Workers' Tools

Along with your mason's hammer, chisels, and level, be sure to stock your stoneworking tool kit with goggles and gloves. It's essential to wear heavy leather gloves when trimming stone, along with the best set of protective goggles you can find. Rock shards will frequently fly off in impossible-to-predict directions, often with great force, so never, ever trim stone without adequate eye protection. Keep children and pets clear of the area, too, lest they become targets of flying rock fragments. ■

Making Changes

One of the advantages of working with dry-stacked stone is that you can make changes later on, as your landscape grows and evolves. Just as we often rearrange and redecorate our indoor rooms, new ideas for our gardens are always germinating, and it's impossible to know which plants or visions will capture our imaginations two, five, or ten years from now.

You will probably find that as your stone skills develop, so do your dreams of how you can use stone in your landscape. The way certain stones host moss in a shady corner may eventually give rise to a moss garden or, if you live in a dry climate, you may become captivated with the shadow dancing of upright stones planted in the soil among water-miser plants. Just because stones are so willing to stay where you put them does not mean that they cannot be moved, rearranged, and changed into something new. Stone may be hard and heavy, but its limits in your landscape are as unbounded as your dreams.

Sedimentary stone such as this layered limestone (LEFT) can be split along the striations with a few well-placed whacks to a chisel with a rock hammer.

Many kinds of stone are difficult to trim or cut by hand (ABOVE). Either accept the chunks as they are or buy pieces that have been cut and trimmed at the quarry.

The Kindest Cuts

Two things are needed to cut and trim stone: patience and reasonably good upper body strength. It is hard, heavy work, but tremendously satisfying as well. Work in short sessions at first, and expect your arms and shoulders to feel stiff the next day — a normal side effect of both impact vibrations and heavy lifting. Not being a Ms. Universe myself, I like to warm up my muscles before swinging a rock hammer with a few minutes of stretching followed by a short session with 8-pound hand dumbbells.

Squaring Off Stone

When building walls, steps, or pillars, you may need to square off cornerstones if you can't find just the right one in your pile of stone. If you've never trimmed stone before, practice trimming on a thin piece before tackling a large, thick stone. Work on a very stable surface, such as the ground or an extremely solid worktable.

Begin by marking the line you want to cut with a pencil or chalk pencil on the top, bottom, and sides. Use a cold chisel and a hammer, with moderate force, to etch a

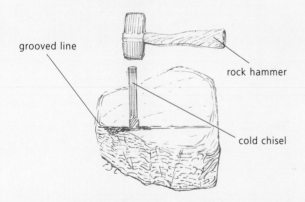

grooved line

rock hammer

cold chisel

groove over the line. Expect the rock shards to fly, and use smaller stones to support the one you're working on as you rotate from one side to the next. It often takes three or more passes to cut a guide groove in a stone.

Now you're ready to get rough. Place the stone so that it is very well supported, with either the top or the bottom facing up, and place the blade of a wide cold chisel in the groove, about an inch from an outside edge. Hit it with as much force as you can, move the chisel down a couple of inches, and keep whacking. The part you are trimming off will usually fall off in chunks. After working down one side, turn the stone over and work down the other. Trim the sides before going back to the top and bottom to trim off ragged edges.

Bumping Off Bulges

Especially with sedimentary stone such as limestone, you may need to remove jagged bulges from the top or bottom of a stone to get it to stack right. With sedimentary stone, you can usually find a natural layer, or striation, beneath the bulge, and then trim back to that layer.

Again, you will need a rock hammer, a cold chisel, and a solid work surface. However, instead of laying the stone flat, prop it up with other stones so that it is diagonal — the best angle for this type of trimming, which is called splitting. Use a 1-inch cold chisel to tap around the bulge with moderate force, which often creates fissures along the vein. Then go back and hit harder, and the bulge should pop off cleanly.

1-inch cold chisel

stone for support

Mortar Matters

Most of the projects in this book involve stacking stone dry, without mortar. Still, you may find situations where you decide that your stonework should be fixed in place, so I'll share the basics of working with mortar and concrete. First, let's look at three terms: cement, mortar, and concrete.

Cement, usually called portland cement, is a chemical blend of calcium, silicon, aluminum, and iron obtained by crushing just the right combination of raw materials, which are then heated to make the chemicals fuse and, finally, pulverized again into a fine gray powder. Cement is an ingredient in both mortar and concrete, and it's what makes the particles in mortar or concrete stick together so that they dry as hard as rock. This is both a physical and a chemical process. In addition to the stiffening that takes place as mortar dries, chemical reactions continue for months, which make the mortar get harder and harder. So it's proper to speak of mortar or concrete as curing rather than simply drying.

Mortar is usually a mixture of cement, lime, and sand, but unless you need a huge amount, it is usually simplest to buy mortar mix, to which you add only water. You can mix small amounts of mortar in a plastic pail or the tub of a wheelbarrow. Mix only as much as you will use in an hour or so, and use only as much water as needed to make a thick, gloppy mixture that does not run. Mortar that is too thin cracks easily after it cures, and a mixture that's too thick is difficult to spread and cures so fast that it's prone to crumbling. Still, it's easier to add more water than to get rid of too much, so start with a little less water than you need and add a few dribbles at a time until you get a smooth yet thick consistency. Be sure to mix the mortar and water thoroughly, so that no dry pockets remain.

Besides adding stability, mortaring the stones in this formal pillar made it possible to get each corner perfectly square.

Whenever you build a stone structure that must be absolutely stable, such as the top of a sitting wall, it's wise to mortar the capstones in place. You can also use mortar to secure the interior parts of a wall, but leave the joints deeply recessed so that the mortar is hidden from view. Mosaics created from small stones benefit from a bed of mortar, too, and some people prefer mortared walkways to those with earth or gravel crevices.

Concrete contains less cement and more sand, so it is less dense than mortar. At home supply stores, you can choose between premixed dry concrete with or without added gravel. Most likely, your main interest in concrete is in how to cover up old concrete with stone. This is best done by cleaning the old concrete, applying a concrete adhesive according to package directions, and then mortaring stone in place.

Concrete also can be used to form a permanent weatherproof footer for a stone wall, or you can build a wood form along a new stone walkway and fill it with concrete to form a permanent edging. Concrete footers or edgings should be allowed to cure for at least three days before the stone portions are added.

Working with Mortar

It's a mistake to assume that you can use mortar as a substitute for having to select and place stones so that they fit together well. True, mortar makes it possible to build with rounded stones, but you must still pay close attention to fit if the structure is to stand the test of time. Another fine point to remember is that mortar that cures slowly is much stronger than mortar that cures quickly.

Because dry stones absorb water, always dampen stones that are being mortared together. If you're repairing old mortar, wet the crevice before you fill it with fresh mortar. Once a mortared structure is complete, lightly spray it with water once or twice a day for four days to slow the curing process. In hot weather, take the added step of covering mortared structures with clear plastic for four days to slow the evaporation of water.

It is worth the effort to be extremely neat when working with mortar, because small bits dry fast to form permanent stains. Work slowly and carefully, and clean up any drips or spills right away with a wet cloth. And although stone walls with thick, almost oozing mortared joints were at one time fashionable, most of us want to see as much stone — and as little mortar — as possible. This means that you will have to "strike" joints by scraping away excess mortar when the stones are laid, and then go back a few hours later to brush out mortared joints with a wire brush. Besides recessing the joints, brushing smooths the texture of the mortar, which is a crucial finishing touch if you want the mortar to be nearly invisible.

Tiers of steps (LEFT) gain additional permanence and stability when constructed with mortar.

The use of mortar (RIGHT) provides the strength needed to raise a retaining wall high into a hillside.

Resources

The plants in this book are easy to grow when given an appropriate site, yet some can be hard to find. Below are some fine specialty nurseries, as well as sources of garden ornaments and water gardening supplies. Even when buying plants mail order, it's best to use nurseries close to home to avoid shipping delays, especially in quarantine states (AZ, CA, OR, WA) where plants can be held several days for inspection.

Plants for Walks, Steps, Walls, and Rock Gardens

Elk Mountain Nursery
P.O. Box 599
Asheville, NC 28802
828-683-9330
Web site: www.elk-mountain.com
From ajuga to mazus, offers creepers, perennials, trees, and native plants

Foliage Gardens
2003 128th Avenue SE
Bellevue, WA 98005
425-747-2998
Web site: www.foliagegardens.com
Specializes in spore-grown ferns, Japanese maples, and Kousa dogwoods

Go Native!
P.O. Box 3631
Las Cruces, NM 88003
800-880-4698 / (fax) 505-522-5080
Web site: gonative.com
Dry-climate native wildflowers and shrubs, plus perennials, ground covers, and herbs for arid regions

Green Glow Nursery
10993 W 550 N
Flora, IN 46929
219-699-6955
Web site: hometown.aol.com/
   hardycacti/
Cacti hardy to Zone 5 that also tolerate high rainfall, plus sedums, ice plants, and other drought-tolerant perennials

JDS Gardens
RR #4, 2277 County Road 20
Harrow, Ontario
Canada N0R 1G0
519-738-9513 / (fax) 519-738-3539
Web site: jdsgardens.com
Huge selection of cold-hardy perennials, ground covers, and plants for walls, crevices, and rock gardens

Mountain Valley Growers
38325 Pepperweed Road
Squaw Valley, CA 93675
559-338-2775 / (fax) 559-338-0075
Web site: mountainvalleygrowers.com
Huge selection of herbs, including creepers, plus many fragrant perennials

Plant Delights Nursery
9241 Sauls Road
Raleigh, NC 27603
919-772-4794 / (fax) 919-662-0370
Web site: plantdelights.com
Perfect perennials for the upper South and Mid-Atlantic regions, or for plant collectors anywhere

Porterhowse Farms
41370 SE Thomas Road
Sandy, OR 97055
Phone and fax: 503-668-5834
Web site: porterhowse.com
Rare conifers by the hundreds, plus suitable small trees and shrubs to go with them

Roslyn Nursery
211 Burrs Lane
Dix Hills, NY 11746
631-643-9347 / (fax) 631-427-0894
Web site: roslynnursery.com
Extensive collection of rare azaleas, rhododendrons, hardy camellias, ferns, conifers, Japanese maples, hostas, and other garden-worthy plants

Shady Oaks Nursery
1101 S. State Street, P.O. Box 708
Waseca, MN 56093
800-504-8006 / (fax) 888-735-4531
Web site: www.shadyoaks.com
A hundred hostas, plus ferns, astilbes, and many other perennials made for the shade

Silk Purse Farm Perennials
115415 Grey Road 3
RR 4, Peabody
Chesley, Ontario
Canada N0G 1L0
Web site: silkpursefarm.on.ca
Organically grown hardy hostas, perennials, and rock garden plants

Siskiyou Rare Plant Nursery
2825 Cummings Road
Medford, OR 97501
541-772-6846 / (fax) 541-772-4917
Web site: srpn.net
A long-standing leader in mail-order rock garden plants

Squaw Mountain Gardens
P.O. Box 946
Estacada, OR 97023
503-630-5458 / (fax) 503-630-5849
Web site: squawmountaingardens.com
*Specializes in sedums and semper-
vivums, along with ferns and dwarf
conifers*

Sunnyboy Gardens
3314 Earlysville Road
Earlysville, VA 22936
804-974-7350
Web site: sunnyboygardens.com
*Many creeping thymes, Corsican mint,
and other herbs for sunny crevices*

Sylvan Nursery
1028 Horseneck Road
Westport, MA 02790
508-636-4573 / (fax) 508-636-3397
Web site: www.sylvannursery.com
*Heathers by the dozen, plus hardy
perennials, trees, and shrubs*

T & L Nursery
13245 Woodinville-Redmond
  Road, NE
Redmond, WA 98052
425-885-5050 / (fax) 425-861-5412
Web site: tandlnursery.com
*Lots of blooming heathers and orna-
mental grasses, ground covers, and
perennials*

Wayside Gardens
1 Garden Lane
Hodges, SC 29695
800-845-1124
Web site: www.waysidegardens.com
*Superior cultivars of hundreds of land-
scape plants, including ground covers
and vines*

We-Du Nurseries
2055 Polly Spout Road
Marion, NC 28752
828-738-8300 / (fax) 828-738-8131
Web site: www.we-du.com
*Native and non-native shrubs, trees,
wildflowers, and perennials adapted to
the humid Southeast, including rock
garden and crevice plants*

Stone Ornaments

If concrete just won't do, and you
long for a genuine stone water bowl,
here are some excellent sources. Stone
is heavy, and shipping it can be costly,
so I've tried to name sources in different parts of the country.

Elegant Accents West
515 Independent Road
Oakland, CA 94621
510-568-6255 / (fax) 510-568-6360
Web site: gardendiscovery.com
*Japanese stone lanterns and bowls; also
bamboo fountains and fencing*

Japanese Style
16159 320th Street
New Prague, MN 56071
877-226-4387 / (fax) 952-758-1922
Web site: japanesegifts.com
*Japanese garden ornaments including
lanterns, bowls, fountains, and bamboo fencing*

Stone Forest
P.O. Box 2840
Santa Fe, NM 87504
888-682-2987 / (fax) 505-982-2712
Web site: stoneforest.com
*Carved granite fountains, lanterns,
bowls, and troughs*

Water Gardening Supplies

The skyrocketing popularity of water
gardening has fueled the emergence of
specialty pond shops everywhere, and
local folks are your best source of
information about aquatic plants
known to grow well in your area. But
small shops may not stock just the
pump or filter you need. The suppliers listed here maintain large show-
rooms and have a proven track record
in the mail-order business.

LaBrake's Garden Path & Pond
8 Pitt Street
Brushton, NY 12916
877-909-5459
Web site: gardenponds.com
*Selection of hardware, accessories, and
plants so vast that it's best studied from
their CD-ROM catalog*

Lilypons Water Gardens
P.O. Box 10, 6800 Lilypond Road
Buckeystown, MD 21717
800-999-5459
Web site: lilypons.com
*One of the oldest and best suppliers of
hardware, plants, and fish, but espe-
cially water lilies*

Van Ness Water Gardens
2460 North Euclid Avenue
Upland, CA 91784
800-205-2425 / (fax) 909-949-7217
Web site: vnwg.com
*One of the original mail-order suppliers
of pond supplies, and still an industry
leader*

USDA Zone Map

The United States Department of Agriculture (USDA) created this map to give gardeners a helpful tool for selecting and cultivating plants. The map divides North America into eleven zones based on each area's average minimum winter temperature. Zone 1 is the coldest and Zone 11 the warmest. Once you determine your zone, you may use that information to select plants that are most likely to thrive in your climate. As an example, a plant that is described as "adapted in Zones 5 to 8" should be able to withstand the cold winter temperatures of Zone 5, as well as the summer heat of Zone 8.

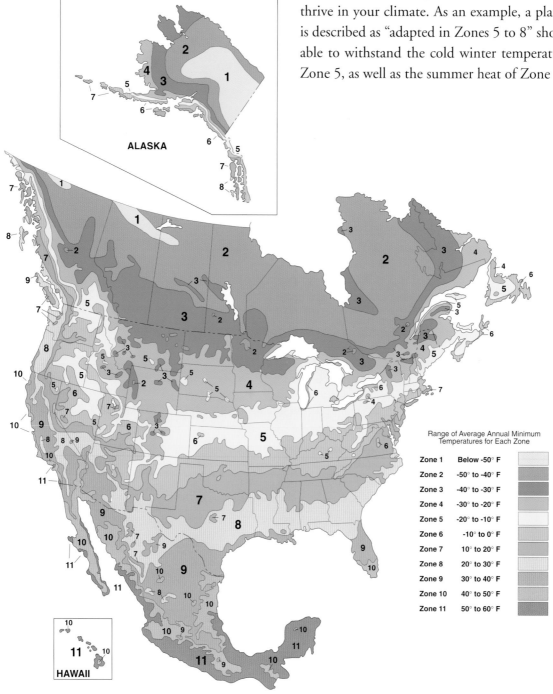

ALASKA

HAWAII

Range of Average Annual Minimum Temperatures for Each Zone

Zone 1	Below -50° F
Zone 2	-50° to -40° F
Zone 3	-40° to -30° F
Zone 4	-30° to -20° F
Zone 5	-20° to -10° F
Zone 6	-10° to 0° F
Zone 7	10° to 20° F
Zone 8	20° to 30° F
Zone 9	30° to 40° F
Zone 10	40° to 50° F
Zone 11	50° to 60° F

Photography Credits

All photos are by Dency Kane, except for the following.

Crandall and Crandall: pages 25 (bottom left), 46, 67, 144, 180, 184. MACORE Company, Inc.: pages 75 (third from top), 76 (second, third, and fourth from top), 157 (third from top). Greg Vaughan/MACORE Company, Inc: page 130 (third from top). Jerry Pavia: pages 89, 173, 177, 188 (top), 189 (second from top).

Barbara Pleasant: pages 33, 42, 65, 85 (middle), 114, 115, 28 (bottom), 131 (top), 203 (bottom right), 219. Positive Images: Jerry Howard, page 10; Margaret Hensel, page 91; Liz Ball, page 145; Pam Spaulding, pages 171, 199. Storey Publishing: Giles Prett, pages 37 (all photos), 76 (top), 126, 166, 187, 189 (bottom), 192, 193 (bottom), 197 (bottom), 207 (both photos), 210, 211, 216 (all photos), 217, 224, 225 (both photos)

Garden Locations and Designers

Front cover: (top) Mark and Leslie Weinberg Garden, Tenafly, NJ; (bottom left) Galerie Waterloo, Winkel, Holland. Back cover: Chateau Barteau, East Hampton, NY. Pgs. v (middle), 101, 191: Chateau Barteau, East Hampton, NY; p. 41 (bottom): Rich Boyd Garden, Nashville, TN; p. 43: Chapellet Vineyard, St. Helena, CA; p. 169 (top): Disney Institute, Orlando, FL; pgs. 107, 196, 209 (right): Epstein Garden, Tenafly, NJ; p. 116: Marla Gagnum Garden, Design by Marla Gagnum of English Landscape Design, East Hampton, NY; pgs. 59, 105, 110, 168: Iva Gillet Garden, Maryland; p. 48: Hester Garden, Princeton, NJ; pgs. 103 (bottom), 111 (bottom), 165, 195: Hidden Pond, East Hampton, NY, Rock Landscape/Design by Richard Cohen and Jim Kutz of Rockwater, Amagansett, NY; p. 122 (bottom): Horkan Garden, Upperville, VA; pgs. 21, 46, 64, 118, 146, 149 (right), 198, 200, 213: John P. Humes Japanese Stroll Garden, Locust Valley, NY; title page, pgs. 19, 34, 35, 51, 80, 85, 111 (top), 140, 178, 182, 185, 206, 214, 215: Innisfree Garden, Millbrook, NY; p. 106 (right): Phyllis Kaplan Garden, Bennington, VT; pgs. 12 (left), 13 (top), 122 (top): Terrance and Saskia Keeley Garden, Amagansett, NY, Landscape Design by Jane E. Lappin, East Hampton, NY, Masonry by Tom Ciccariello and Mike Ruddy, Seven Sons, Inc., Montauk, NY; p. 172: Kenilworth Gardens, Asheville, NC; p. 40: Keukenhof Garden, Lisse, Holland; pgs. 120, 154, 229: Longwood Gardens, Kennett Square, PA; p. 27: Carol Mercer Garden, East Hampton, NY, Design by Carol Mercer and Lisa Verderosa, East Hampton, NY; p. 62: Mohonk Mountain House, New Paltz, NY; p. 102: Morris Arboretum, Philadelphia, PA; pgs. 22 (top), 52: Morris/White Garden, San Antonio, TX; p. 164: Mt. Cuba Center, Greenville, MD; pgs. 137, 152: Wendy Nelson Garden, Boonesville, MD; pgs. 133, 138, 155: The New York Botanical Garden Rock Garden, Bronx, NY; p. 136: Elaine Peterson and Richard Kahn Garden, Montauk, NY; p. 161: Private garden, East Hampton, NY, Design by Jim Grimes of Fort Pond Native Plants, Montauk, NY; pgs. 9, 134, 135, 203 (bottom left): Private garden, Greenwich, CT, Design by Carrie Maher Greenwald and Mark Greenwald, Stamford, NY; pgs. 20, 31 (bottom left), 92: Private garden, Memphis, TN, Design by Ben Oke; pgs. 13, 148: Private garden, Boston area, MA, Design by Shiro Nakane with Julie Moir Messervy; p. 151: Private garden, Wellesley, MA, Design by Julie Moir Messervy; p. 31 (top): Private garden, Water Mill, NY, Design by Diane Sjoholm of Sirius Design, Sag Harbor, NY; pgs. 32, 84, 108, 163: Private garden, Bridgehampton, NY, Design by Diane Sjoholm of Sirius Design, Sag Harbor, NY; pgs. 124, 227: Private garden, Greenwich, CT, Design by Edmund D. Hollander and Maryanne Connelly of Hollander Design, New York, NY; p. 15: Rice Garden, southern Vermont; p. 58: Dean Riddle Garden/Designer, Lanesville, NY; pgs. 203 (top right), 208 (bottom): River Farm, Alexandria, VA; pgs. 36, 81, 119: Diane Sjoholm Garden, North Haven, NY, Design by Diane Sjoholm of Sirius Design, Sag Harbor, NY; p. 70 (top): Sparkill Labyrinth, Dominican Center, Sparkill, NY; pgs. 72, 109: Lee Stoltzfus Garden/Designer, Lititz, PA; p. 16: Van Vleck Garden - Designer Showcase, Montclair, NJ, Design by June Bonasera of Montclair, NJ; p. 39: Van Vleck Garden — Design Showcase, Montclair, NJ; p. 190: Martin Viette Nursery, East Norwich, NY; p. 167: Walsh Nurseries, Dix Hills, NY; pgs. 56, 203 (top left): Galerie Waterloo, Winkel, Holland; pgs. 11, 30, 197 (top): Mark and Leslie Weinberg Garden, Tenafly, NJ; p. 70 (bottom left): Wisdom House Labyrinth, Litchfield, CT, Design by Barbara Putnam, Litchfield, CT

Metric Conversion Chart

When the measurement given is	To convert it to	Multiply it by
inches	centimeters	2.54
feet	meters	0.305
mils	millimeters	0.254
square feet	square meters	0.093
ounces	grams	31.1
pounds	kilograms	0.373
tons	metric tons	0.907
gallons	liters	3.785
°F	°C	°F − 32 x $\frac{5}{9}$

Index

Note: page numbers in *italics* indicate photographs or illustrations.

A

achillea, *9*

acorus, *15*

Aethionema grandiflorum. See stonecress

ageratum, 109

ajuga (*Ajuga reptans*), 46, 74, *74,* 96, *96,* 137, *140,* 174

alpine clematis (*Clematis alpina*), 128, *128*

alpine heather. *See* spring heath

alpine liverwort (*Erinus alpinus*), 75, *75*

Androsace lanuginosa. See rock jasmine

annuals, 111, 123, 175, 188

Arabis species. *See* rock cress

Armeria maritima. See sea thrift

artemisia, 73

artistic effects, 204–205, *204, 205,* 210–211, 225

Athyrium nipponicum 'Pictum'. *See* Japanese painted fern

Aurinia saxatilis. See basket-of-gold

azalea, 115, *119,* 151

B

Bacillus thuringiensis, 187

backyards, 58–59, 108

bamboo, 149, 200–201, *201*

barberry, *31*

basalt, 34, *37,* 42, 43, *43,* 135, 211

base of walkways, 48–49, 62–63

basil, 73, 116

basket-of-gold (*Aurinia saxatilis*), 109, 128, *128*

batter, 104, *105,* 113, 127

bearded iris, *30*

beginners' projects, 102, 173

bellflower (*Campanula* species), 74, *74*
    C. elatines var. *fenestrellata,* 74, *74*

benches, stone. *See* seating

bermuda grass, 63

Betula nigra. See river birch

bitterroot (*Lewisia rediviva*), 158

blazing star (*Liatris*), 111

bleeding heart, *145*

bloodroot (*Sanguinaria canadensis*), 154

Blue Atlas cedar, *155*

blue phlox (*Phlox divaricata*), 51, 154

bonsai, 149

borage, 117

Boston ivy (*Parthenocissus tricuspidata*), 111, 153

boulders, 82, 86, *165, 193, 197, 207. See also* seating
    use of, in garden design, 26–29, *27, 31, 43*
    working with existing, 150–151

boxwood, *23*

brick, 46–47, 50, 63

bridges, 95, *95*

bronze fennel, 117

bugleweed. *See* ajuga

bulbs, 71, 109, 111, *115, 135,* 137, 139, 143, 145, 153, 158

bunchberry (*Cornus canadensis*), 96, *96, 194*

C

cactus, 25, *141,* 159, *159, 196*

cairns, 208, *208*

Calluna vulgaris. See heathers

Caltha palustris. See marsh marigold

Calycanthus floridus. See Carolina allspice

Campanula species. *See* bellflower

candytuft (*Iberis sempervirens*), 46, 109, 111, 129, *129,* 142

capstones, *103,* 106–107, *106, 107,* 113, *113,* 127, *127,* 143
    on sitting wall, 120–121, *121,* 228

Carolina allspice (*Calycanthus floridus*), 123

carpenter's level, 54, *54,* 55, 63, 68, 87, 89
    to install a pond, *170*
    to level a sitting wall, 121, *121*
    to measure run of steps, 83, *83*

carpet bugle. *See* ajuga

carving stone, 38–39, 210–211

catmints (*Nepeta* species), 143

cattails, 176

cement, *68,* 177, 187, 227

centaurea, *110*

Cercis canadensis. See redbud

checkerberry. *See* wintergreen

chemicals
    in drinking water, 169
    for weed control, 63, 73

cherry trees, 109

chin cactus (*Gymnocalycium* species), 159

Chinese gardens, 19, *19, 85*

chisel, 53, *53,* 210, 211, *224, 225, 226,226*

chives, 73, 117

Christmas fern (*Polystichum acrostichoides*), 155

chrysanthemums, 149, *149*

cinnamon fern (*Osmunda cinnamomea*), 155

cinquefoil, 51

clematis, 123, *207*

Clematis alpina. See alpine clematis

cleome, *58*

cliff maids (*Lewisia* Cotyledon Hybrids), 158, *158*

climbing rose, 153

cobble (cobblestones), 24, 50, 57, 58, 63, *63,* 87, 88

columbine, 51, *154*

concrete, 112, 228

conifers, *196, 198*

coping stones, 170, *170,* 175

coreopsis, 143

Cornus canadensis. See bunchberry

Corsican mint (*Mentha requienii*), 60, 76, *76*

Cotoneaster horizontalis. See rockspray cotoneaster

crabapple trees, 109

cranesbills (*Geranium* species), 51, 75, *75*

Crataegus species. *See* hawthorns

creeping dogwood. *See* bunchberry

creeping juniper (*Juniperus* species), 25, 109, *209*

creeping myrtle (*Vinca minor*), 89, 99, *99,* 109, 115

creeping oregano (*Origanum vulgare* 'Compactum'), *72,* 73, 76, *76*

creeping phlox (*Phlox subulata*), 89, 98, *98, 103,* 109, 130, *130,* 197

creeping rosemary (*Rosmarinus officinalis* cultivars), 117

creeping rues, 151

creeping thyme (*Thymus* species), 73, 98, *98,* 117, *117,* 150
    T. polytrichus, 98, *98*
    T. praecox ssp. *arcticus* 'Albus', 117, *117*

creeping veronica (*Veronica prostrata*), 99, *99*

crevices, filling or planting, 50–51, 55, 73, 74–77, 87, 127
   among boulders, 151
   with herbs, 117, *117*
   with mosses, 155
   in retaining walls, 112–113, *113*
   in water gardens, 169, 174

crushed rock. *See* paver base

cultivator. *See* pronged hoe

curly parsley, 73

cutting stone, 53, 224–226

D

daffodils. *See* narcissus

daisies, *145*

daphne, *138*

daylilies, *13, 95,* 111, 142, *142, 207*

dead nettle. *See* lamium

Delosperma species. *See* ice plant

delphinium, *10*

desert stone, 25

desert varnish, 25

designing
   for multiple levels, 78–99
   with stone, 16–25
   walkways, 46–47, 60, 196
   water gardens, 162–165

dianthus (*Dianthus* species), 73, 75, *75,* 109, 123, 129, *129,* 197
   D. gratinapolitanus, 129, *129*
   D. microlepis, 75, *75*

Dicentra cucullaria. See Dutchman's breeches

ditches of stone, 92–95, *92, 93, 95*

dowsing rod, 71

drainage, 116, 140
   ditches, *92, 93*
   pipe, 50, *50,* 90, 91, *91,* 108, 118
   solutions, 50, 90–95, 118, 119

drains
   French, 90, 92
   Japanese surface, 91, *91*

dry-laid
   stone steps, 84
   walkways, 47, 48–55

dry-stacked stone, *102,* 114, *114,* 115, *115,* 225

dry well, 50, *50*

dusty miller, 73

Dutchman's breeches (*Dicentra cucullaria*), 154

dwarf annuals, 109, 142

dwarf apricot, 209

dwarf basil, 73

dwarf cattail, 175

dwarf daffodil, 71, 158

dwarf iris, 154

dwarf Japanese maples, 177

dwarf lotus, 175, 187

dwarf mondo grass (*Ophiopogon japonicus*), 76, *76*

dwarf ornamental apricot trees, 109

dwarf parsley, 117

dwarf pines, 148

E

Echinacea purpurea. See purple coneflower

Echinops chamaecereus. See peanut cactus

edging, 50–51, 63, 65, 66, 85, 89, 142

end stones, 106

English ivy (*Hedera helix*), 46, 97, *97,* 109, 115

English roses, 123

entrances, 46, 196–197, *196, 197*

Erica carnea. See spring heath

erosion, 40, 96

Escobaria vivipara. See "little" cactus

estimating
   stone amounts, 217
   volume of water, 179, 183

Euonymus fortunei. See wintercreeper

Euphorbia myrsinites. See myrtle spurge

euphorbia, *140*

evergreens, 148, 176, 207, 209

F

fences, with walls, 124–125, *124, 125*

ferns (numerous species), 95, 99, *99,* 115, 119, *120, 127,* 131, *131,* 150, 177, *185, 198*
   in woodland gardens, 154, *154,* 155, *155*

fertilizers, 138–139, 157, 159, 189

fieldstone, *17,* 48, *70,* 217
   definition of, 36

filters and pumps, 166–167, *166, 167, 172,* 179

pump ratings, 183
   water quality, 187

fish, in water gardens, 162, 164, 169, 170, *171, 173, 177,* 187

flagstone, *23,* 38, 42, 46, 50, *52,* 57
   definition of, 40
   scoring and trimming, 53

flowering cherries, 148

flowering plums, 148

flowering tobacco (*Nicotiana* species), 123

foamflower, 154

fossils, 36, 106, 204–205

foundations
   of house, and retaining walls, 109
   for retaining walls, 112–113
   for rock garden, 136
   for stone steps, 86–87, *86*
   for walkways, 48–49, *49,* 54

fountains, *161*

foxglove, 51, *155*

framing stone steps, 84, 88–89

free stone, 217

freezing of soil, 49, 73, 112

G

Galium odoratum. See sweet woodruff

gardenias, 123

garden walls, 110–111, *110*

Gaultheria procumbens. See wintergreen

gayfeather, *191*

Genista pilosa. See prostrate broom

Geranium maculatum. See goosefoot geranium

Geranium species. *See* cranesbills

goatsbeard, *9*

golden thyme, 117

goosefoot geranium (*Geranium maculatum*), 154

granite, 34, *37,* 42–43, *42,* 65, *111,* 135, 199, 200, 211, *225*

grasses, 95, 177. *See also* lawns *and* turf

gravel. *See* processed gravel *and* gravel gardens

gravel gardens, 64–65, *64, 65*

grotto walls, 118–119

ground covers, 46, *60,* 95, 109, 114, 115, 197

Gymnocalycium species. *See* chin cactus

H

Hamamelis species. *See* witch hazel
hawthorns (*Crataegus* species), 127
heathers *(Calluna vulgaris)*, 145, 157, *157*
Hedera helix. See English ivy
helianthemum (*Helianthemum nummularium*), 157, *157*
heliotrope, 123
hen-and-chicks. *See* sempervivum
herbicides, 63
herbs, 193
   as crevice material, 51, 73
   in garden beds, 116–117, *116, 117*
   with retaining walls, *109*
heucheras, *119, 120, 154*
hills and dips, using stone in, 78–99
honeysuckle, 123, 124, *142*
hostas (*Hosta* species and cultivars), 115, *119*, 129, *129*
houseleeks. *See* sempervivum
hyacinths, 123
hypertufa, *186*, 187

I

Iberis sempervirens. See candytuft
ice, melting, 73
ice plant (*Delosperma* species), 129, *129*
   D. cooperi, 129, *129*
igneous rock ("fire rock"), 34, 42–43
impatiens, *22, 114*, 115
indigenous stone. *See* native stone
injury. *See* safety
Ipomoea batatas. See sweet potato vine
iris, *95*, 142, *143*
Iris laevigata, I. pseudacorus, I. virginica. See water iris
Irish moss. *See* pearlwort
ivies, 150, *197*

J

Japanese gardens, 20–21, *20, 21, 64, 146–147, 146, 193*, 198
Japanese maple trees, 109, 149, *149, 209*
Japanese painted fern (*Athyrium nipponicum* 'Pictum'), 99, *99*
Japanese spiraea, 209
Japanese spurge. *See* pachysandra
Japanese surface drains, 91, *91*
juniper (*Juniperus* species), *95*, 109, *209*

K

kamchatka stonecrop. *See* stonecrop

L

labyrinths, 69, *69, 70*, 71, *71*
lamium (*Lamium maculatum*), 89, 97, *97*
landscape design, 16–25, 57
landscaping fabric, 52, 63, 94, *94*
lanterns, stone, 198–199, *198, 199*
lava rock, 166, 199
lavender, *13, 122, 123*, 145
lawns, walkways for small, 59. *See also* grasses *and* turf
ledge gardens, 143
lettuce, *12*
level. *See* carpenter's level
lewisia (*Lewisia* species), 158, *158*
Lewisia Cotyledon Hybrids. *See* cliff maids
Lewisia rediviva. See bitterroot
Liatris. See blazing star
lichens, *10*, 25, *31*, 154, 197, 215, *215*
lifting. *See* safety
lighting, 85, 126, *126*, 173
lilies, 142
limestone, 34, 36, 37, *37*, 40, 57, *106, 111*, 121, 200, 204, 210, *225*, 226
liners, installing, for water gardens, 168–171, *171*, 180, *180*, 184
lines, in garden design, 29, 105, 110, 199
ling. *See* heathers
liriope, 46, 115
"little" cactus (*Escobaria vivipara*), 159
lobelia, 71, 109, 142
locating
   container water gardens, 186
   herb beds, 116–117
   rock gardens, 134–135
   stone benches, 192
lotus. *See* water lotus

M

magnolias, hardy deciduous, 109
Mammilaria. See cactus
marble, *37*, 40, 41, *41*
   chips, 41
   in gravel gardens, 65
marsh marigold (*Caltha palustris*), 188, *188*
Marsilea mutica. See water clover

M (continued)

mason's hammer, 68, 224, *224*
mason's trowel, 153
materials
   mixing, in walls, 111
   for steps, 84–85
   for stepping-stones, 62
Matteuccia struthiopteris var. *pennsylvanica. See* ostrich fern
mattock, 112, 141
mazus (*Mazus reptans*), 98, *98*
meditation, 69–71
Mentha requienii. See Corsican mint
metamorphic rock, 34, 40
mints, 116, 117, 193, *193*
moraines, 141
mortar, 227–229, *228, 229*
   replacing, 153
   for sitting walls, 121
   with stone, *35, 42, 47, 63, 63, 107, 168*, 180, *180, 227*
   in tree wells, 115
mosaics in stone, 66–68, *67*
moss (numerous species), *31*, 36, 118, 119, 131, *131*, 150, 151, 154, 215, *215*
   as crevice material, 51, 68, 155
moss pink. *See* creeping phlox
moss rose, 145
moss verbena, 85, 111, 145
mother-of-thyme. *See* creeping thyme
mountain, creating miniature, 144–145
Mount Rushmore, 211
moving stone, 215, 218–223
mulch, as crevice material, 51, 57
   in labyrinth sites, 71
   for rock gardens, *138*, 139, 150
   as winterizing material, 73
multiple levels, designing for, 78–99
myrtle spurge (*Euphorbia myrsinites*), 97, *97*

N

narcissus (*Narcissus* species), 111, 142, 153, 158, *158*
nasturtiums, 117
native (indigenous) stone, 16, 19, 24
Nelumbo species. *See* water lotus
Nepeta species. *See* catmints
Nicotiana species. *See* flowering tobacco
Notocactus haselbergii, 159, *159*

nutrients, for rock garden plants, 138–139
nutsedge, 63
Nymphaea species. *See* water lily

O

obsidian, 42
Ophiopogon japonicus. See dwarf mondo
   grass
Opuntia humifusa. See cactus
opus vermiculatum, 66
oregano (*Origanum* species), 117
Oriental poppies, *110*
Origanum majorana. See sweet marjoram
Origanum species. *See* oregano
Origanum vulgare 'Compacta'. *See* creeping
   oregano
ornamental grasses, *163*
ornaments, garden, 190–211, *191, 203,*
   210–211, *210, 211*
Osmunda species. *See* cinnamon fern *and*
   royal fern
ostrich fern *(Matteuccia struthiopteris* var.
   pennsylvanica), 131, *131*

P

pachysandra *(Pachysandra terminalis),* 46,
   98, *98,* 109
panel planting, 109
parrot's feather, 162
parsley, 73
Parthenocissus species. *See* Boston ivy *and*
   Virginia creeper
Parthenocissus tricuspidata. See Boston ivy
pathways. *See* walkways
paver base (rock dust), 49, *49, 50,* 54, *54,*
   55
   as base for stepping-stones, 62, 63
   as base for stone steps, 86–87, *86, 87,* 89
pavers, 42, 65, *70*
paving stone, 48, 49, *49, 50,* 57, *60, 70,*
   73, *86,* 217
pea gravel. *See* processed gravel
peanut cactus *(Echinops chamaecereus),* 159
pearlwort *(Sagina subulata),* 76, *76,* 174
peat moss, 51, 68
penstemon *(Penstemon* species), 145
peonies, *109, 137,* 142
perennial plants, *110,* 111, *135, 175,*
   188–189
   in panel plantings, 109
   for tree wells, 114, 115

winterizing, 73
periwinkle. *See* creeping myrtle
permission to remove stone, 33
Persian candytuft. *See* stonecress
petroglyphs, 211
petunias, 85, 109
phlox, 51. *See also* blue phlox *and* creeping
   phlox
Phlox divaricata. See blue phlox
Phlox subulata. See creeping phlox
photographs, for reference, 153
pillars, 126–127
pinks. *See* dianthus
Pistia stratiotes. See water lettuce
placement of stone, 55, 57, 206, 208
planning, 217, 218, 220
   in building walkways, 48–51
   in garden design, 26–29, 207
   of gravel gardens to be raked, 65
   for a mosaic, 68
   for steps for slopes, 82
   walls, 102–103, 110–111
      with fences, 125
   water gardens, 168–169, 173
planting stones, 206–208, *206, 207, 208*
plants
   among boulders, 151
   in crevices, 72–73, *72,* 74–77, 112–113,
      113, 214
   as edging for stone steps, 85, *85,* 89
   as edging for walkways, 50–51, 196–197
   for fragrance, 72–73, 122–123
   in garden design, 30–31, 46
   in labyrinths, 71
   for pillars, 127
   for rock gardens, 134–135, *134, 135,*
      140, 156–159
   for ruins, 153
   for stepped rockery, 143
   for steps and swales, 96–99
   for walls, 102–103, *102, 103,* 128–131,
      219
   for water gardens, 162, 169, 175, 176,
      177, *177, 181,* 187, 188–189
plywood, 55, *55, 68,* 175
pocket ponds, 166, 172–175, *172*
poly foam, 180
Polystichum acrostichoides. See Christmas
   fern
ponds and pools. *See* water gardens
portland cement, 187, 227

portulaca, 145
preparation of site
   for gravel garden, 64–65
   for mosaic, 68
   for scree garden, 141
   for stepped rockery, 143
   for walkway, 48
   for water gardens, 169
primrose *(Primula* species), 145, 158, *158*
   P. sieboldii, 158, *158*
Primula species. *See* primrose
processed gravel, 49, *49, 50,* 54, *54,* 65,
   89, 91, 118
   as base for retaining walls, 112–113,
      112
   as base for stepping-stones, 62–63, *63*
   as base for stone steps, 86–87, *86, 87,*
      88–89
pronged hoe, 65, 141
prostrate broom *(Genista pilosa),* 151
pry bar, 55, 61, 73, 206, 215, 221, 222,
   222, 223, 223
pulmonaria, 115
pumps. *See* filters and pumps
purple coneflower *(Echinacea purpurea),*
   143

Q

quack grass, 63
quarries, *216, 218*

R

raised beds, 116
raking patterns, in gravel gardens, 65
rebar stakes, 89, *89,* 112, 120, 151, 201
recycled stone, 42
redbud *(Cercis canadensis),* 127
reinforced risers, 89, *89*
retaining walls, *15, 108, 163, 191, 229*
   building, 112–113, 217
   for multiple levels, 81, *81*
   for slopes, 108–109, *108, 109,* 196
rhododendrons, *24,* 95, 115
rise of steps, measuring, 83, *83*
riser
   measuring, 83, *83*
   stones, 86, *86,* 87, *87*
   wood as, 88–89, *89*
river birch *(Betula nigra),* 127
rivers of stone, 92–93
river stones, *58,* 62, 63, *67,* 71, 177

rock cress (*Arabis* species), 137, 145, 156, *156*
  A. caucasia 'Variegata', 156, *156*
rock dust. *See* paver base
rock gardens, *18,* 20, 132–159, *132, 152*
rock hammer, 210, 211, *225, 226*
rock jasmine (*Androsace lanuginosa*), 151
rockrose. *See* helianthemum
rock shelf, 169, 170, *170*
rock soapwort (*Saponaria ocymoides),* 130, *130*
rockspray cotoneaster (*Cotoneaster horizontalis*), 108–109
rock vs. stone, 33
rosemary, 73, 117
roses, *10, 45, 106, 122,* 123, 124, 177
Rosmarinus officinalis cultivars. *See* creeping rosemary
royal fern (*Osmunda regalis*), 155
rudbeckia, *13*
ruins, stone, 152–153, *152*
run, measuring, 83
runner beans, *58*

S

safety, 86, 219, 224, 225, 226
  with natural hazards, 152, 153
  of walkways, 46, 68
sage, 73, 117
Sagina subulata. See pearlwort
salt, use on walkways, 73
sand, as base
  for mosaic, 68
  for stepping-stones, 61, *61,* 62, 63
  for water gardens, 168, 171
sandstone, *37,* 38–39, *39,* 40, *67, 111,* 121, 135, 199, 200, 210, *211,* 224
Sanguinaria canadensis. See bloodroot
sanvitalia, *58*
Saponaria 'Bressingham'. *See* soapwort
Saponaria ocymoides. See rock soapwort
Satureja montana. See winter savory
saxifrage (*Saxifraga* species), 145, 158, *158*
  S. cotyledon, 158, *158*

scale
  of stone walls, 104–105
  use of, in garden design, 26–29
scented geraniums, 116, 123
Scotch heather. *See* heathers

scree garden, 140–141, *140, 141*
sculpture, with limestone, 36
sea lavender, 95
sea thrift (*Armeria maritima),* 151, 157, *157*
seating
  stone benches, 192–195, *190, 192, 193, 195*
  walls as, 120–121, *120*
sedimentary rock, 34–39, *34,* 40, 42, 150
  scoring and trimming, 53, 224–225, *225,* 226
sedum (*Sedum* species), *9,* 77, *77,* 130, *130, 135, 140, 141,* 145, 150, 151, 174, *185,* 197
  as crevice material, 51
  in rock gardens, 159, *159*
  S. sieboldii, 139
  S. spectabile, 111
  S. spurium, 77, *77,* 130
  in sun, 111
  in tree wells, 115
Sedum kamtschaticum. See stonecrop
Sedum spurium. See sedum
seed stones, in labyrinths, 71
sempervivum (*Sempervivum* species), *141,* 145, 151, 159, *159*
setting
  stone steps, 86–87
  stone in walkways, 54
shale, *37,* 40, 41, *111,* 211
Shasta daisy, *110*
shims, 61, 87, 113, *113,* 170, 177, 193, 206
shredded bark, 62
shrubs, *124, 135, 144, 175,* 176, *191,* 209
Siberian catmint, *108*
Siberian iris, *11*
side yards, *56,* 57, 108
site preparation. *See* preparation of site
size
  of plants for rock garden, 136
  of stones, 104, 119, 124, *147,* 196
sizing of steps for multiple levels, 81
slabs, 84, *84, 85, 185, 195*
slate, *37,* 40, 41, *111, 195*
slopes
  considerations regarding, 57
  and drainage, 90
  and effect on rock garden, 136

moving stone down, 220–221
  and tree wells, 115
  use of steps on, 80–89
  and walls, 102, 196
  and water gardens, 166
snowbell, 209
snowdrops, 71
soaker hose, 115, 139
soapstone, 210, *210*
soapwort (*Saponaria* 'Bressingham'), 77, *77*
soil
  mixes, for rock gardens, 138–139, 141
  in tree wells, 114
  type, for plantings in crevices, 112–113, *113*
  in wall foundations, 112
spotted deadnettle. *See* lamium
spring heath (*Erica carnea*), 157, *157*
stachys, 51
statues. *See* ornaments, garden
stepped rockery, 142–143, *142*
stepping-stones, *21,* 28, *48,* 56, *57,* 58, *59,* 60, 61, *61, 67,* 95, *213*
  embedding, 62–63, *62*
  in gravel gardens, 64–65, *64*
  in water gardens, 176, *177*
steps, stone, *29, 35, 41,* 57, *79, 85,* 195, *228*
  setting, 86–87
  use for multiple levels, 80–89, *80, 81*
stinging nettle, 152
stone
  about, 32–43
  bowls, 145
  buying, 33, *33,* 38, 43, 215–217
  cutting and trimming, 53, 224–226, *225, 226*
  groupings, 208, *208*
  moving, 215, 218–223
  positioning, in walkways, 55
  ruins, 152–153
  special (keepsake), 197, *197*
  walls, 100–132, *101, 108, 109*
  working with, 212–229
stonecress (*Aethionema grandiflorum*), 156, *156*
stonecrop (*Sedum kamtschaticum),* 130, 159, *159*
stone hammer, to cut stone, 53, *53*
straw, as winterizing material, 73, 139

stream gardens, 178–181, *178*
striking joints, 229
style, in garden design, 19–25
succulents, 25, *31, 36*, 129, 159
sunrose. *See* helianthemum
swales, 92–95, *94*
sweet alyssum, 71, 109, 123, 142, 145
sweet marjoram *(Origanum majorana)*, 117
sweet potato vine *(Ipomoea batatas)*, 130, *130*
sweet woodruff *(Galium odoratum)*, 73, 75, *75*
symbolism of plants, 148–149

T

tamping tool, 54, *54*
'Tapien' verbenas. *See* verbena
tea ceremony, 199, 200–201
thresholds, 126–127, 176, 195
thrift. *See* sea thrift
thyme, *72,* 73, 89, *122,* 197
Thymus polytrichus. See creeping thyme
Thymus praecox ssp. *arcticus* 'Albus'. *See* creeping thyme
Thymus pseudolaniginosus. See woolly thyme
tie stones, 105
toad lilies, 154
torenia, 115
trailing myrtle. *See* creeping myrtle
transporting stone, 33
tread
    measuring, 83, *83*
    stones, 87, *87*
tree roots, 115, 180
trees, 109, 209, *209*
tree wells, 114–115, *114, 115*
trilliums, 151, 154
tulips, *115,* 142
turf, 60–61. *See also* grasses *and* lawns
types of stone, 34–43

V

variegated dogwood, *191*
verbena *(Verbena* hybrids), 131, *131, 191*
    'Tapien' verbenas, 131, *131*
Veronica prostrata. See creeping veronica
veronica *(Veronica* species), 145
viburnums, 209
vines, 111, 119, 123, 124, 154, 207, *207,* 215
Vinca minor. See creeping myrtle
vining ground covers, 115
violets, 151, *154*
Virginia creeper *(Parthenocissus quinquefolia),* 111
volcanic rock. *See* igneous rock

W

walkways, 44–77, *45, 46, 48,* 73, 174, 176–177, *213*
walls, stone, 100–132, *101, 105, 106, 107, 214. See also* fences *and* retaining walls
water
    estimating operating volume of, 179, 183
    in Japanese gardens, 147, 200–201
    for moraines, 141
    recirculating, 201, *201*
    for rock gardens, 136, *136,* 139, 144
    for tree wells, 115
    in woodland gardens, 154
water bowls, of stone, *22, 36,* 68, 118, *118,* 199, 200–201, *200, 201, 211*
water clover *(Marsilea mutica),* 189, *189*
waterfalls, 162, *162, 163, 167,* 182–185, *184, 185*
water gardens, 162–189, *164, 165, 168, 169, 171, 172, 173, 175, 181, 182, 186*
watering, in gravel gardens, 65
water iris *(Iris virginicia, I. laevigata, I. pseudacorus), 15,* 175, 176, 188, *188*

water lettuce *(Pistia stratiotes),* 189, *189*
water lilies *(Nymphaea* species), 162, 175, 187, 189, *189*
water lotus *(Nelumbo* species), 162, 189, *189*
    N. nucifera, 189, *189*
water problems. *See* drainage
weed control, 52, 63, 71, 73, 94
weight of stone, 219
width
    of steps, 81
    of walkways, 58–59
wildflowers, 154
wild violets, 51
willow, 149
wintercreeper *(Euonymus fortunei),* 109
wintergreen *(Gaultheria procumbens),* 97, *97*
winter hardiness, 123
winterizing walkways, 73
winter savory *(Satureja montana),* 117
wisteria, 123
witch hazel *(Hamamelis* species), 123
wood. *See also* fences
    as form for pads, 63, *63*
    as frame for stone steps, 84, 88–89
    as riser material, 88–89
    as walkway edging, 50, 63
wood chips, with stepping-stones, 62
wood hyacinth, 115
woodland gardens, 154–155, *154*
woodland rues, 154
wood sorrel, 51
woolly thyme *(Thymus pseudolaniginosus),* 77, *77*

Y

yuccas, 25

Z

Zen gardens, 65, 147

Other Storey Titles You Will Enjoy

Outdoor Stonework: 16 Easy-to-Build Projects for Your Yard and Garden, by Alan and Gill Bridgewater. A complete primer on working with stone, with instructions on choosing materials, safety considerations, and cutting and fitting techniques. Projects include flagstone steps, retaining walls, a cantilevered seat-shelf, and more. 192 pages. Paperback. ISBN 0-8266-976-1.

Stone Style: Decorative Ideas and Projects for the Home, by Linda Lee Purvis. Incorporate the natural tones and textures of stone into your life with projects and ideas from gifts to home accents to indoor garden features. 128 pages. Hardcover. ISBN 1-58017-375-6.

Deckscaping: Gardening and Landscaping On and Around Your Deck, by Barbara W. Ellis. Landscaping instructions, planting techniques, and decorating tips for strengthening the links between your home, your deck, and your surrounding garden. 176 pages. Hardcover. ISBN 1-58017-408-6.

Natural Stonescapes: The Art and Craft of Stone Placement, by Richard Dubé and Frederick C. Campbell. With this start-to-finish guide, anyone can design and build stone groupings modeled after geological formations found in nature. Practical tips for choosing stones and more than 20 sample designs are included. 176 pages. Paperback. ISBN 1-58017-092-7.

Step-by-Step Outdoor Stonework: Over Twenty Easy-to-Build Projects for Your Patio and Garden, edited by Mike Lawrence. From walls, arches, patios, paths, steps, rock gardens, and fountains to seats, tables, sundials, and birdbaths, this book provides complete instructions for adding attractive stone features to your garden. 96 pages. Paperback. ISBN 0-88266-891-9.

Stonescaping: A Guide to Using Stone in Your Garden, by Jan Kowalczewski Whitner. Learn to build garden features with enduring stone, including steps, walls, paths, ponds, and rock gardens. Features 20 basic designs. 168 pages. Paperback. ISBN 0-88266-755-6.

Stonework: Techniques and Projects, by Charles McRaven. Learn to collect and handle stone while creating walls, stairs, pools, and waterfalls. 192 pages. Paperback. ISBN 0-8266-976-1.

Building with Stone, by Charles McRaven. An introduction to the art and craft of creating stone structures with step-by-step project instructions. 192 pages. Paperback. ISBN 0-88266-550-2.

Building Stone Walls, by John Vivian. Includes equipment requirements, instructions for creating wall foundations, information on coping with drainage problems, and hints for incorporating gates, fences, and stiles. 122 pages. Paperback. ISBN 0-88266-074-8.

Build Your Own Stone House Using the Easy Slipform Method, by Karl and Susan Schwenke. Complete instructions on tools, materials, estimating, siting, excavating, and using stone, and removing forms. 176 pages. Paperback. ISBN 0-88266-639-8.

These books and other Storey books are available at your bookstore, farm store, garden center, or directly from Storey Books, 210 MASS MoCA Way, North Adams, MA 01247, or by calling 1-800-441-5700. Or visit our Web site at www.storey.com.